MIKE SPENCE
OUT OF THE SHADOWS

Mike at the 1966 British Grand Prix. *Reading Evening Post/John Spence*

First published September 2021
Copyright Text copyright Richard Jenkins
Page layout and graphics copyright Performance Publishing Ltd

ISBN 978-0-9576450-9-7

Author Richard Jenkins
Designer Sarah Scrimshaw

Front cover Main image: Pete Darley
Rear cover Sigurd Reilbach

Printed by The Manson Group Ltd, Hertfordshire AL3 6PZ

Publisher Performance Publishing Ltd
Unit 3 Site 4 Alma Park Road,
Alma Park Industrial Estate,
Grantham, Lincolnshire NG31 9SE, Great Britain

Mike at the German Grand Prix, 1964. *Etienne Bourguignon*

Mike Spence and Malcolm Angood. *Lynne Spence*

Dedicated to the memory of
Malcolm Ralph Angood
27 November 1942 to 27 November 2020
A great friend to Mike and Lynne Spence
A mechanical wizard who helped contribute to this book

Mike Spence (2) and Jackie Stewart (1) line up on the grid for the 1964 Rand Grand Prix in their Lotus 33s. A few seconds later, Stewart's race would be over.
Ken Stewart/David Pearson (www.motoprint.co.za)

There has been very little written about Mike and I am pleased to see that this has been rectified with this book which explores deeply both Mike's personal life and his racing career and helps bring Mike out of the shadows into a focus he now deserves.

My experience with Mike was one of friendship as well as driving against him in my early years of entering Formula One. In fact, my first ever Formula One race was at the Kyalami Race Track near Johannesburg in South Africa, when Colin Chapman called me at the end of November to ask if I would drive alongside Mike Spence in the grand prix, a two-part race which at that time was quite common. I had already signed with BRM so explained that this would not be practical or possible. He asked whether it might be possible if he obtained permission from BRM for me to drive the car, as Jimmy had slipped a disc throwing snowballs when he was helping Ford to launch the Lotus Cortina in Cortina in Italy and was unable to drive, as was intended. In addition to which, I was also to stand in for Jimmy at the same meeting driving a Lotus Cortina at Kyalami.

BRM allowed Chapman to have me for that one event and ironically I put the car on pole with Mike beside me on the grid, also in his works Lotus. The driveshaft broke on the start line, however in the second part of the grand prix, I started from the back of the grid and won that race. Graham Hill was the overall winner and Mike finished second in the first heat, before retiring in the second heat with a broken suspension rod.

Mike Spence was a true gentleman with very generous good manners, he presented himself extremely well, and was much loved in the Formula One community. I suppose the biggest problem was that he was driving a Lotus at the same time as Jim Clark, who Colin Chapman clearly cared for in the most intensive fashion, which often, I fear, did not offer the best opportunities for Mike or the No2 Lotus drivers.

I sincerely hope this book will give many people an inside look to a lovely man, who was modest to the end.

Sir Jackie Stewart OBE

There are not many two-time Formula One race winners that have not merited a published biography of any description. Mike Spence was, until this book, one of them. Maybe this is because he was, generally, a modest, quiet man in a largely conceited and thunderous sport, or perhaps because he was eclipsed by the many strident individuals he worked with. Maybe it is because his two wins were non-championship victories and not World Championship races. But Mike's life is a story well worth telling and he had a career that is worth revisiting.

As with the subject of my first book, Richie Ginther, Mike has somewhat been forgotten. At the same time, like Richie, just the mention of his name meant, to the right audience, a number of memories regarding the man, the cars he drove and the races he competed in, came flooding back. It is also worth noting the quantity and quality of the names involved with contributions to this book and the author of the foreword to this book – not from a 'look at how great the author is' point of view, but rather the esteem that Mike was held in by his peers. Not one person remembered Mike in any negative connotation and the warmth and fondness he was held in by many shone brightly through.

No further introduction to Mike was needed on most occasions other than his name. But while I am happy to be the motorsport literature's somewhat patron saint of forgotten racing drivers, it is important to state that there should be no real comparisons between Richie and Mike, other than I am the author of both of their books. They raced against each other and were both quite brilliant development drivers. They both have a back story that deserves more in-depth coverage. But the two men were very different personality-wise and had very, very different outcomes in terms of their death.

Mike was, at his death, one of Britain's best racing drivers and there is an argument that during the time he raced in Formula One, Mike was one of the top five British drivers, only behind the four World Champions of Clark, Hill, Surtees and Stewart. Without wanting to then start a discussion of whether Mike was better than Bob Anderson, Peter Arundell and Innes Ireland, to name just three, what was clear was that Mike was very much in demand in both Grand Prix racing and in the sports car world. His opportunities were opening up for him before tragedy intervened.

His career of just under ten years is covered extensively with my hope that this biography brings Mike into the forefront somewhat, for the first time. The reason for the title of the book is that, during the vast majority of his career, Mike, largely due to his polite and laconic nature, was overlooked and his achievements, especially with the development and

The author and Lynne Spence, July 2020. *David Martin*

mechanical sympathy he showed all his racing cars have somewhat been lost. If you look purely at statistics, Mike Spence is a non-qualifier at the Indianapolis 500. Racing alongside such deservingly feted legends like Jim Clark and Jackie Stewart obscured all the groundwork Mike did to support his famous Scottish teammates.

As much as this book is about Mike, the era Mike raced in is an iconic one and as such, I have tried to provide a bit of background and context to Mike's career through the personalities, machinery and championships of the time. A mere glance at the race results of 1967's Formula One season, for example, do not explain why, despite finishing no higher than fifth, Mike's stock was quite possibly at its very highest that year. As with Richie Ginther, I hope that the net result of this biography is a fresh look at Mike's very notable achievements in the sport.

I have many people to thank for their assistance with this book. Sadly, one of them, Mike's former mechanic Malcolm Angood, did not live to see this book published and a dedication to his memory is on the early pages.

In alphabetical order of surname, I would like to thank: John Adams, Lesley Appel, Richard Attwood, Julian Balme, Darren Banks, Chris Beach, Eric Biggadike, Arthur Birchall, Bruce Boembeke, Keith Booker, Etienne Bourguignon, Helen Bramley, Rick Braverman, Allen and Susan Brown, Bill Cowe, Mark Crawley, Bob Dance, Peter Darley, Donald Davidson, Peter Davies, Roger Dixon, Tony Dron, John Fenning, Adam Ferrington, Walter Fooshee, the Formula Junior Historic Racing Association, David Fox, Kevin Guthrie, Jim Hall, Richard Heseltine, David Hobbs, Vince Howlett, the Indianapolis Motor Speedway, Paul Jeffrey, Mike Jiggle, Raimund Kommer, Karl Ludvigsen, George Levy, Mark Lowrie, Gary Magwood, Dai Martin, Jim Meikle, Sarah Mitrike, Iain Nicolson, Doug Nye, Michael Oliver, W Alec Osborn MBE, Richard Page, David Pearson, Jim Pickles,

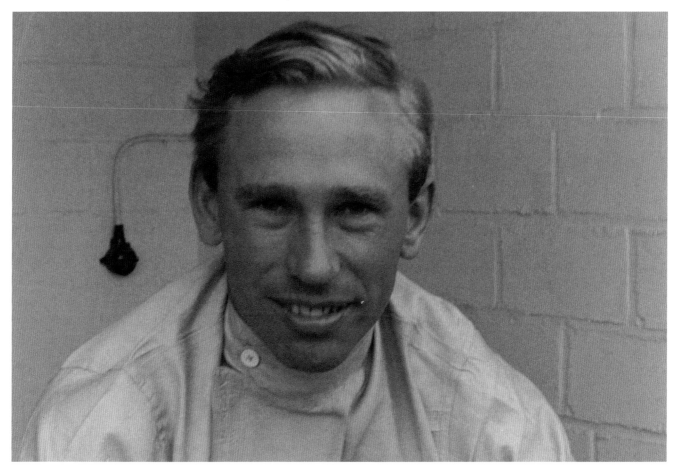

Mike at the Belgian Grand Prix, 1965. *Etienne Bourguignon*

David Piper, Peter Procter, Graham Rabagliati, Alan Rees, Sigurd Reilbach, Alan Rigarlsford, Nils Ruwisch, Richard Scammell MBE, Cedric Selzer, Mervyn Silver, John Sismey, Joe Skibinski, Bob Sparshott, Rene Speur, Simon Stiel, Ady Stimpson, Judy Stropus, Andy Talbot, Les Thacker, Todd Treat, David Tremayne, Ian Wagstaff, Ted Walker, Emma Watts and Paula Willis (and all at Classic Team Lotus).

I also want to thank the following editors for allowing me to use previous articles and quotes from their respective publications; Phil Bell (*Classic Cars*), Kevin Turner (*Autosport*) and Gordon Cruickshank (*Motor Sport*).

I am very thankful and honoured that Sir Jackie Stewart has written the foreword for this book and I sincerely thank him and his team for the time they have invested in this book, despite, even with coronavirus restrictions, an extremely busy schedule.

Special thanks must be reserved for two more people. One of them is Mike's brother, John, who now lives in Australia. John sent many emails and a whole litany of photographs, including very special family photographs which help give this book a really personal feel. The other is Mike's widow, Lynne, now Lynne Martin.

Lynne, who is an indefatigable force of nature, has embraced the project with more enthusiasm and support than I ever dared envisage. Together, we have helped each other give you, the reader, a thoroughly detailed and revealing insight into what was essentially a quite private man. The journey through writing this book brought back some terrible lows for Lynne but it has also brought some wonderful highs and I am greatly pleased that this project has brought her back into contact with so many of her friends from that time and has been, overall, a positive experience for her.

To wrap this introduction up, thanks to my publisher, Adam Wilkins, who was completely supportive during this process, as he always has been with anything I've suggested. I consider our win with the Ginther book for the Royal Automobile Club Book of the Year 2020 to be as just as much his triumph as it was mine. It is a real pleasure to work with someone so enthusiastic and dedicated. Thanks, too, to Sarah Scrimshaw for her design work with this book, making it out to be the visual treat I believe it is.

My final thanks go both to my supportive family and to my wife Amy, who through good and bad, is always there to support me. Thank you my love for everything you do.

Purley King

"Ever since I was a child, all I wanted to
do was to become a racing driver"
Mike Spence, 1968

Mike Spence and his brother John (in car), 1941. *John Spence*

ichael Henderson Spence was born on the penultimate day of 1936, a dry winter's day, at the Hutton Nursing home that was located in Pampisford Road near the border of South Croydon and Purley, which is on the outskirts of London. The nursing home is now an assisted living residence which, as it was in 1936, is linked to the Purley and District War Memorial Hospital which is based more or less opposite the nursing home. The very first fallacy often repeated about Mike was that he was born in Croydon, but his birthplace should really be listed as Purley.

The unusual moniker of Henderson as Mike's middle name was a family tradition passed down many generations of his paternal family. His father, David, a mechanical engineer, as well as David's brothers Arthur and James, all had Henderson as their middle name, as did all of Mike's paternal-great aunts. The original Henderson was Janet, Mike's paternal great-grandmother from Scotland.

Mike's brother, his only sibling, was named after his uncle and his father. John David Spence arrived on 10 July 1939. John Spence described the sibling relationship to me as "Always good, but he was always one step ahead of me in life and we did not do much together after he left school."

John Spence filled out a bit more of the family history in his autobiography written for his family and friends. Grandpa Spence (James, who was born in 1869) started as a draper's assistant working with his father in a fabric shop in the Glasgow area. He also lived in Kirkcaldy before moving to a slightly more exotic base. He moved to Paris to study the fashion clothing industry and this is where he met his future wife. Around the turn of the century, the Spence family moved to Surrey, where they had six children; five sons and one daughter. The youngest of the sons was Mike's father David, who was born on 22 September 1909.

A very young Mike Spence. *John Spence*

James earned his fortune in the clothing and fashion industries. By his retirement, James and his wife Annie were able to employ four servants at their home in Kenley; a cook, a parlour maid, a chauffeur and the chauffeur's wife. In the latter part of his career, James became a successful fashion buyer for major shops and then became the deputy chairman of the Debenhams group of stores.

Grandpa Goddard, father of Mike's mother, Winifred, started work with his father's hardware shop before using his training and experience to move into manufacturing and subsequently became the founder of a company called British Trolley Track Ltd, which made tracks for sliding doors. Both grandparents were financially successful and were able to offer their children a good education and they were also able to buy homes in a fairly exclusive area in Surrey.

The Spence family lived in the large family home, The White House, in Court Hill, Chipstead, Surrey (where John was born), which was, and indeed still is, an affluent area. Mike's father ran the sliding door engineering and construction business which was now called Coburn Engineering, based in nearby Kenley. John Spence takes up a little bit of the background to the firm: "Our father's first employment was in the Midlands, around the Staffordshire/ Derbyshire area, and Mike was nearly born there. Shortly before his birth, my mother's father, Mr Goddard, asked

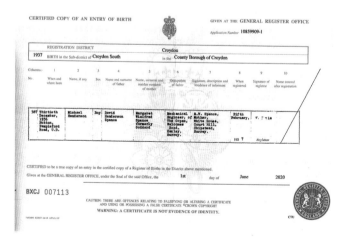

Mike Spence's birth certificate *Richard Jenkins*

The Spence family home – The White House, Chipstead. *John Spence*

The Spence family on holiday. From left to right: Mike, David, John and Winifred Spence, 1950. *John Spence*

him to come down south to take over the running of British Trolley Track Company, which later on had its name changed to Coburn Engineering." Before that move, David was working for a company that produced dyed silks.

Although there is no question that James, David and Mike all worked hard, family money was available for anyone to indulge in a variety of interests. When James died in 1955, he left £275,000 in his will. In 2020, the equivalent amount would be £6.5million.

All was well for the first few years of Mike's life, but two events would shatter the harmony the Spence family enjoyed. The first was the onset of World War Two. Anything on the periphery of London's outskirts was an automatic target for the German Luftwaffe bombers and, as the *Sutton and Croydon Guardian* reported in 2012, a startling 1343 high explosive bombs and parachute mines were dropped over the Croydon area between October 7 1940 and June 6, 1941.

John Spence, although born just months before the outbreak of World War Two, has, perhaps only naturally, vivid memories of the war years. "We were still living in Chipstead throughout the war. Once I had recovered from my stomach surgery [Author note: This is explained more later], the plan was for us all to move down to a holiday home owned by Grandpa Goddard not far from Plymouth, right on the River Yealm. However, our father received call-up papers for military service. Then our mother's brother John was also called up. When the factory was taken over by the War Department, either John or our father had to run the factory and one had to serve in the military. As our father had children and John did not, John went into active service. He later served in North Africa and gained the Military Medal for gallantry in Tobruk, before spending two years in a prisoner-of-war camp in Italy.

"Our father was released from the armed forces so he could run the factory producing tank tracks located just near London Bridge station. A bomb shelter, a bit more sophisticated than the Anderson, was built in our garden and one of my earliest memories is of us playing 'I Spy' by the light of a single red bulb in the little concrete cavern. Of course, there was very little to spy in this cave-like structure! Originally, our very first shelter was under the solid oak dining table which was under the stairs of our home. Other memories include watching with Mike as a Spitfire tipped the wing of a V1 flying bomb to send it off course. One landed at the end of our road demolishing several houses and causing minor damage to our home. I also well remember making Christmas decorations with the aluminium 'window' dropped by the German bombers so to confuse their radar. We also kept ducks, grew vegetables and even picked rose-hip berries to make rose-hip syrup, which of course helped with rationing, not just for us but for the community." Although Chipstead was more rural and smaller than many of the other suburbs nearby, it was still just fifteen minutes away and still very much in the flight path of the incessant bombers.

Then, in the summer of 1942, there was disaster when Mike was struck down by poliomyelitis. Although polio does still exist, the development of a vaccine in the 1950s largely eradicated the disease from most countries. In 2020, it was announced that the disease is no longer prevalent in Africa and is now in only two countries in the entire world; Pakistan and Afghanistan. It's hard, these days, to remember what devastating effects polio could have. The disease at its peak in the 1940s and 1950s, caused largely by ingesting contaminated food or water, paralysed or killed over half a million people worldwide every year. The more recent

Tepstede, the Spence's second family home with the long gravel driveway used for billy-cart racing! *John Spence*

John and Mike Spence at John's wedding in 1962. *John Spence*

Mike works on the family Riley Imp. *John Spence*

coronavirus has brought back some memories for those who remember polio at its peak.

The disease hit without warning, totally indiscriminate as to who it afflicted, with long quarantine periods during which parents were separated from children. If they survived, polio victims were normally affected for life, with the disease attacking the muscles of the body and its nervous system. Paralysis was common, but withered or deformed limbs also occurred while, in some serious cases, iron lungs were used as a ventilator to aid breathing.

Dependent on which publications you read about Mike's polio fight, he was either near death, or spent a long time trying to overcome the disease. One of the more dramatic recollections of Mike's polio battle was that 'the surgeons and doctors said to his devastated parents that he had little hope of survival and even less hope of emerging from the disease without paralysis.' Another colourful 1960s magazine article refers to Mike even having a disability.

John Spence puts it far more subtly in context. "Mike contracted a mild case of polio which left him with a slight limp for some time but fortunately nothing more." In fact, the Spence child closest to death was arguably John, who when had a defective valve in his stomach at birth and was unable to feed. Given just days to live, he survived an operation aged just eleven days, but it was a close run thing.

It took Mike about six months to remove the limp but it left no long-term effects physically, and nor did it affect him mentally. In fact, it was almost as if it never happened. Mike's wife Lynne later said that had she not known that he had polio in the past, she would not have noticed it, whereas John, his brother, added "I never saw any physical limitation or saw him have any medical check-ups." After all, when you look at it in context, Mike was just five years old and, like so many other children of that age, seemed to bounce back from mortal danger without a care or worry in the world.

The AC Bristol 1959 001. Mike racing the AC Bristol at the 35th BARC Members' Meeting, Goodwood, 6 June 1959. *John Spence*

In fact, as John Spence pointed out, the closest Mike came to peril was probably via the hands of life-long friend David Porter: "Mike nearly had his skull split open – accidentally – by David Porter swinging a hoe back over his head while we were digging a trench to protect ourselves from a supposed stone throwing gang from up the road. Our road was unmade and largely covered in chalk with the occasional bit of flint so ammunition was plentiful! Mike's scalp needed some stitches but fortunately no more. He would have been about eight years old at the time."

According to cousin Jim Meikle, in his book, *All Set From a CERT*, written in 1962 to cover the first three years of Mike's Formula Junior career, Mike and David [Porter, who he knew from nursery school and was Mike's best friend] 'Have long shown an interest in competition, starting with some alarming descents of the drive at Chipstead when he and David piloted home made vehicles down, round the centre rose bed and into the road. Inevitably, the karts spent a large proportion of their time in the workshop which is significant as today Mike thoroughly knows the inside of the cars and does a lot of work himself. This mechanical knowledge is of very great value when diagnosing faults or determining gear ratios.' John Spence also remembers a young David well. "We were in comparative isolation through the war years. The Porter family across the road had an older son, David, who was the same age as Mike so we became friends and played war games, built a camp in the wood and our first billy-cart. In 1952 we moved to a house backing onto the golf course with quite a long downhill driveway covered in small gravel. The billy-cart was fitted with some springs, a brake and roll restraints. If you managed two curves near the bottom with minimal braking you emerged onto the road, which was fortunately a cul-de-sac, at a fair speed."

John Spence then takes up the narrative of his brother's childhood and adolescence. "After the war, Mike went off to Brunswick boarding school [which no longer exists] and in 1946 I joined him. However, I think Mike was picked on by a teacher there and that could have been why, in July 1946, my parents took him out of Brunswick and at the age of nine he went to a new day school called St Christopher's [which also no longer exists], which was based one station stop down the railway while I, aged seven, stayed at Brunswick. After he changed schools we only had holidays together.

"After the war the family MG saloon was resurrected and we would help our father with the maintenance, including jobs like decoking the engine. We both gained a fair mechanical knowledge. Our father was a keen and very good golfer and so we learned golf. Mike was left-handed but with no left-handed golf clubs he had to play right-handed. I think this may explain why, when playing cricket,

Mike in the prototype of his uncle's rear engined sports car, the Zanzara Special, which was based on Mini Cooper. It was never completed as Mike progressed rapidly in his career. *John Spence*

he bowled left-handed but batted right-handed. He became the first school captain at St Christopher's and in 1950 went on to St Edward's in Oxford. I am not sure why they chose St Edward's, possibly because cousin Jim Meikle went there a year or two earlier. Our uncle, Dr Jim Spence, lived quite close by, so this may have been a bit of a comfort blanket for Mike in his first boarding experience since he left Brunswick." Jim Meikle offers a further explanation about the choice of St Edward's: "I was there at the same time as Mike but I had an elder cousin that also went to St Edward's so I think it was just a natural family thing that if one child goes somewhere, the others, if they choose to, follow. The school knew of the wider family and we knew the school."

Mike very nearly chose cricket as his sporting pastime. He played for his school at St Christopher's and then at St. Edward's, at Oxford. John Spence: "In 1950, Mike's ability in cricket was in part developed by a two-day coaching event at his primary school run by Alec and Eric Bedser. [Author note: Alec (later Sir Alec) and Eric Bedser played first-class cricket for Surrey for some 20 years. Alec was one of England's finest post-war cricketers.]

"Mike became the opening bowler for the school cricket team. Colin Cowdrey, who was then captain of the English test team visited the school. [Author note: Colin Cowdrey, later Baron Cowdrey of Tonbridge, was one of England's finest ever cricketers. He was the first cricketer to play 100 test matches and, at the time of his retirement after 21 years of test cricket, he was the most prolific Test batsman, holding a record of the most test centuries by an Englishman until 2013. As a mark of his greatness, he was only the fourth, and currently last, sportsman to be honoured with a memorial service at Westminster Abbey.]

"Well, Colin Cowdrey came to give a coaching session, and during that, Mike clean bowled him, gaining quite a reputation." Mike's move away from cricket came largely through his time in the national service (more of which is below). It must also be mentioned that Mike was in the school's second team for rugby.

According to Max Le Grand's profile on him in *Small Car* magazine in 1964, Mike was thought to be a 'bright lad' at St Edward's School at Oxford. However, he was considered even brighter by his peers, when he founded a school motor club there. John Spence however says, academically, Mike was not brilliant. "Mike was an average student at school but always had good practical skills – we both used to make balsa wood flying model aircraft but before the days of both radio controls and glow plug engines, it was a frustrating hobby."

Jim Meikle agrees: "Mike was a bit shy, but enthusiastic child. Very athletic. He was always taking part in something athletic. But academically, he was not at the top range." Mike himself mentioned, casually, that mathematics and science were probably his strongest subjects in a few interviews.

Mike was always a motor racing fan as he recalled to the *Reading Evening Post* in April 1968: "Ever since I was a child, all I wanted to do was to become a racing driver. I was a big fan of Juan Manuel Fangio as I grew up." Mike, once he was old enough to drive, would often travel to Goodwood, Silverstone and his favourite track, Brands Hatch, to watch the racing. John Spence: "We used to attend club races at Goodwood when the circuit was open after the war. Two years later Mike gained had his driver's licence and our father bought a Standard-engined Morgan 4/4 and our mechanical experience increased.

In 1954, the Morgan was exchanged for a 1935 Riley Imp that claimed to be 'ex Freddie Dixon' [Author note: Freddie Dixon was a pre-war racing driver and a significant modifier of racing cars, notably Rileys] with twin SU carbs and some

work to lighten it. Mike left school in 1955 and was called up into the Army based at Catterick in Yorkshire, where he started taking part in club rallies. With him away, I effectively inherited the Imp, which I used until just before my marriage in 1962 when it was sold to a friend who was an industrial chaplain in the Church of England. It helped show him to be, in his words, 'a normal person'! He returned it to near original condition after spending over 20 years on it and I recently saw a photo of it at the Bicester Heritage Centre. It had played a significant part in Mike's interest in driving rather than cricket."

John Spence moved to Australia in 1971, where he still lives today with his wife Christine and their ever-growing family. He has spent most of his working life in education, initially starting as a science teacher in Preston, Lancashire, before working in a town called Miami in Queensland. He then moved to Brisbane before becoming deeply involved in the teaching and management of a Christian school on Queensland's Gold Coast. John also spent some time working as a volunteer in Beira, Mozambique, to help support a school in a destitute suburb progress in a number of areas, including literacy. As a committed Christian, John's life took a very different path from Mike's but the pride he took from his brother's achievements in racing were obvious to see in our correspondence.

Mike in the Turner 948cc BMC at the 36th BARC Members' Meeting, Goodwood, 27 June 1959. *John Spence*

Mike continued to use the AC Ace for transport. It's parked up here by the caravan and transporter. Mike's Emeryson Formula Junior car is in the foreground with (left to right) Winifred Spence, John Spence (hidden), David Porter and Leo Ackroyd by the car. *Mike Spence/Lynne Spence*

A relaxed Mike enjoys a break from racing. *Lynne Spence*

John Spence concludes: "From 1957 onwards, I was stationed in Anglesey, some 10 hours away, and we did not have much time together from then on. I rarely saw him compete, partly because I am not a good spectator and there was an understanding that my parents did not want both of us taking the risk. Mike come up to visit several times and caused quite a stir arriving in a red Ferrari. But there was not a great following for motor racing in that area and I was never touched by having a famous brother."

Mike, like most of his generation, had to serve two years of National Service, and he spent his in Germany. If there was any further proof that the polio had a negligible effect, it was the fact he was passed as A1 to serve. He is listed in numerous publications as a tank commander, but in fact this probably was not the case.

His brother, John, said, "There was little opportunity for cricket in Germany, which was another reason that fell by the wayside and racing took over. From what he told me, he spent most of the time as a driver in the Austin Champ scout cars which were powered by the Rolls-Royce designed engine and it had excellent cross-country performance. He may have driven tanks but never told me of this." His wife Lynne also doesn't think Mike drove tanks. "All he would tell me about Germany was that he had a lot of fun driving this jeep [the Champ scout car] and that the camaraderie was fantastic, but one day he saw a friend of his squashed by a tank against the wall and that was the end of the discussion of his time in National Service."

John Spence fills in a bit more. "Mike came back in 1957 and, in same year, the family Coburn factory was moved to Peasmarsh near Godalming and we moved to Coopers Bridge, a seven-acre property in Bramshott near Liphook. This was

Mike's base when he was racing the AC and the Turner, and where they built the Formula Junior Cooper. Mike lived there until my parents migrated to Australia in 1963. My uncle, who ran the factory with my father, was also keen on cars and they decided to build a rear engine sports car based on Mini Cooper parts."

A few magazines and newspapers report a conversation, no doubt supplied by Mike, between him and his father around 1958, where Mike decided that he wanted to race. His father did not stop him, but understanding what his son wanted in life simply said "What you must do, you must do." Soon, many other members of the wider Spence family were involved in a much more detailed car-building project to help Mike, which would eventually set him on his way to the top echelon of motorsport.

Dead CERT to Succeed

"The car's assembly was carried out by guesswork, common sense, a memory of the chassis seen at Cooper and a small cutaway drawing from *The Motor*"

Jim Meikle, Mike Spence's cousin and mechanic

Mike in the Formula Junior Race at Silverstone, 15 July 1960. *Ted Walker*

Mike started his career somewhat for relaxation. He worked as a sliding door gear engineer in the family firm during the week, taking the YPL 50 number-plated AC Ace-Bristol out for a spot of cobweb-blowing at the weekend. David Spence owned a Turner 950 when Mike was learning to drive and Mike enjoyed the car so much, he took it rallying. The AC Ace-Bristol was purchased specifically by the family for Mike's 21st birthday so that he could compete in racing, although this was with the caveat that it would not be raced regularly and not too seriously.

John Spence gives a bit more background to Coburn and Mike's initial forays in the sport. "By the time Mike was demobbed in 1957, I had won a Flying Scholarship while in the Air Cadets at school, which provided flying training to private pilot's level. I had also gained entry to Cambridge, doing National Service in the RAF in a ground role. With these factors in mind it was understood that Mike would work at Coburn Engineering where he could also pursue his love of competitive driving while I would have the opportunity for study at university and would then make my own way into employment. The factory was moved from London to a larger and more open site near Godalming. My father and uncle wanted to diversify the firm's activities to include fibreglass and, as an experiment, I built a fibreglass punt for a little lake in the grounds of our new home near Liphook.

"The company went on to win a contract to make 'goes under' mechanics trolleys for the Post Office. Mike received his AC Ace-Bristol sports car for his 21st birthday and fitted this with three Weber downdraft carburettors fed by a fibreglass scope which was added to the bonnet. It made him quite competitive in club races at Goodwood and then at other circuits. Our father had bought a Turner sports car to commute to the factory and, when he changed it to a later model, it was fitted with the fully developed BMC engine as fitted to Formula Junior cars, and painted in white with a British Racing Green stripe down the middle. Mike raced this widely competing with the Austin-Healey 'Frogeye' Sprites. They were faster in the dry but Mike's wet track skills put him ahead in the rain. The next step was to try to move to open-wheelers and the only way he could afford to do this was to build his own car, so a crate was delivered containing all the bits for a Formula Junior Cooper/BMC. There were no instructions so Mike and a few other people, but mainly our cousin Jim Meikle, found how to put it together. The firm's Commer van was fitted with a track and pulley system allowing the car to be lifted and just slid inside, and towing a rather old caravan they could travel to the tracks all over the UK where Mike's performances began to be noticed."

Mike and his cousins all joined up to buy Mike a Formula Junior car for 1960 under the Coburn Engineers Racing Team (CERT) banner. Mike had a close-knit team which worked with him for a long time in various guises. David Porter was his business manager and later co-director at Mike Spence Ltd, which was Mike's business that he would later establish. More on that is detailed in the book later on.

Mechanic Malcolm Angood was at this time working at Emeryson, but soon became part of the CERT fraternity and later joined Mike at Ian Walker Racing and then later also worked at Mike Spence Ltd. Angood recalled how he became inextricably intertwined with Mike: "I was an apprentice at a water company when I left school but then a friend of mine mentioned that there was a tuning job going at Emeryson in Send, near where I lived. So I applied for that, got the job and then went to work there. Mike then came in one day and this was the first time I met him. He bought the car and, subsequently, one thing led to another really. I went to a few meetings with him and Mike said 'Do you want to look after the car?' Well, I much preferred going motor racing than being in the workshop, so I said yes!"

Before we go into the trials and tribulations of CERT's debut year of racing, it's worth remembering what Formula Junior actually was and why it was so popular. It was summarised well by motoring journalist Mike Lawrence in *Motor Sport* in 1985, to mark 25 years since the beginning of the series. 'The inaugural season saw the greatest flowering of driver talent of any formula at any time. Twenty of the participants went on to become grand prix drivers, seven won grands prix and three became World Champion. Even the list of those who did not make Formula One is impressive as it includes two rally champions, a multiple sports car champion (Ken Miles) and a multiple touring car champion (John Whitmore).

'Furthermore, no formula has ever created so much excitement among car builders. By the end of 1960, over one hundred different types of car had been constructed for Formula Junior, with the majority purpose-built for the formula and were offered from sale. The speculative customer could choose from around seventy different marques with sixteen different makes of engine, with cars either built rear-engined, with the engine in front of the front axle line and even with the engine mounted alongside the driver. It was a formula that represented a clean sheet of paper whereon all theories could be tested. The formula represented a new phase in the development of the British racing car industry.'

The background to Formula Junior was thus. The 500cc Formula Three races in Britain were hugely popular for drivers and spectators alike, but there wasn't a real equivalent on mainland Europe. In 1957, former racing driver-cummotorsport administrator Count Giovanni 'Johnny' Lurani conceived a relatively inexpensive single-seater formulae that would give young talented drivers a reasonably fair and competitive way to showcase their skills, as 500cc had done for the British drivers.

The other objective Lurani had was to produce a new generation of Italian drivers. By the end of 1957, Italy's leading drivers had either retired (Farina, Taruffi, Villoresi) or were dead (Castellotti, Ascari). Lurani's plan worked, with the likes of Lorenzo Bandini, Ludovico Scarfiotti and Giancarlo Baghetti all progressing to become winners of grands prix. Although there were a wide range of technical rules and opportunities to develop and experiment with cars, procedures were put in place so that, in theory, one car should not be miles ahead of the others and that driving skills would come to the fore.

In the end, Formula Junior effectively, for a few years, gained immense importance. The seismic change came when Formula One moved to 1500cc in 1961 and the old Formula Two 1500cc championship ceased to exist. Formula Junior certainly further launched the upwards career trajectory of Jim Clark and significantly helped the progress of Lotus, Lola and Elva as racing car constructors. Eventually, costs increased and it became very clear that, without a Lotus car, it would be difficult to progress effectively, so the grids rapidly became much smaller than in the inaugural British season of 1960. As well as this, the teams at the front were extremely professional, employed the latest technology and had a huge advantage over the masses of eager amateurs at the back.

At the end of 1963, Formula Junior was split into two categories that replaced it – cars with 1000cc racing engines became the revised Formula Two series and Formula Three was made up of those with 1000cc stock engines.

Peter Procter, a former cycling champion who would later become a very successful touring car driver before his career ended prematurely after being badly burnt in a serious crash in 1966, raced against Mike in Formula Junior and Formula Two. He remembers that Formula Junior was very much a category that was taken seriously: "Formula Junior was very competitive. The cars were good to drive, handled pretty well and were very quick. In fact, it's surprising how quick

Mike in the CERT Cooper BMC at Brands Hatch, 1960.

Lynton Money/John Spence

they were. I go these days to the historic events at Silverstone because of my British Racing Drivers' Club membership and I watch the historic Formula Junior races, and they are very quick, as quick as they were back then. The historic racers of today drive them as we did back then with proper racing. In Formula Junior, you had two types of racers. There were the ones who used the series as they were actively looking to progress in their career, and then there were the amateur racers who were racing for the fun of it and had absolutely no aspirations other to enjoy themselves and do the best they could. Despite that mix, the races were always very competitive, even if people were in it for fun. All the drivers had a lot of respect for each other, no matter what their aspirations were."

John Fenning, who raced with Mike in the same Formula Junior team in 1963, agrees: "Formula Junior was an extremely good series, very competitive with a much smaller pool of drivers than the phenomenal list now. Back then, in 1960 in Hampshire, you could count the amount of racing drivers on one hand. Certainly, Formula Junior beat the hell out of racing on the roads. Everyone aspired to race in Formula Junior. It was very much the open-wheel series to be in, and because most of the top aspiring drivers were in it, it was an extremely good yardstick to one's ability."

Hugh Dibley, a fine driver who enjoyed sports car success but only made racing a hobby as he was first and foremost a pilot for British Overseas Airways Corporation (BOAC), raced in Formula Junior for three years. Dibley recalled to *Motor Sport* magazine in 2018 what Sir Stirling Moss had said to him about Formula Junior. 'You Formula Junior blokes come into a corner five abreast and all want to come out of the corner in the lead. We grand prix drivers are much more civilised.' He was right. They were rather more professional. I used to leave my car on its trailer at the Heathrow crew carpark and then return after a couple of weeks away, in Australia or somewhere, knock the rust off it and go racing.'

Some idea of just how popular Formula Junior was to aspiring racers and constructors is shown by the entries for the Monaco Formula Junior race of 1960. There were 22 spaces on the grid and a colossal 150 entries for the race, with only 50 of those being accepted for the qualification heats. The reason the formula was so popular was accessibility for the amateur, but also because it was a pretty cheap way for the factory teams to enter a competitive series and still get the generous start and prize money that was offered. It also allowed their junior drivers proper race training in a very cut-and-thrust environment. Factory teams took full advantage to enter a number of young drivers to assess their ability.

Malcolm Angood adds the other advantages for both factory teams and exuberant amateurs from a technical

The Coburn Engineering Commer van and transporter.
Mike Spence/Lynne Spence

The transporter on duty. *Mike Spence/Lynne Spence*

point of view. "The Formula Junior cars were very easy to set up from a mechanical point of view. They weren't over complicated. Mike was very mechanically adept and gave good feedback. It was such an advantage for him and for us because it was such a massive help to have someone in the car who knows what it takes to make changes and developments."

In 1962, Mike's cousin, Jim Meikle, put together a book called *All Set From a CERT*. It is partly the true story of the Coburn Engineers Racing Team, but it is also part promotion material and part tongue-in-cheek. When I spoke to Jim 58 years later, he was keen to point out the book was a bit of light-hearted fun and really for the family to share and enjoy. David Porter, for example, describes himself as 'A master tactician, second only to Alfred Neubauer (the legendary Mercedes team manager), and who wears a similar hat'. However it is a very useful guide to the early days of Mike's racing and I as pointed out to Jim, that records of that time are far from plentiful, so it isn't just a useful tool for myself with Mike's racing career, it's a handy tome for a snapshot of the era as it actually was.

It's probably best to quote from the book initially how the project all began. 'After several years of watching racing from the stands and enclosures, a desire was felt to see the thing from the other side of the fence and to participate. During the winter of 1959, ways and means were discussed and plans were finally formulated with a view to taking part seriously.

'The plan was to form the Coburn Engineers Racing Team and to race a Formula Junior car and a modified Turner during the season; finance was to be split three ways between Mike Spence, Keith and Wendy Hamblin [Author note: Wendy was another of Mike's cousins] and Richard Barneby. Mike and his men were to maintain the cars throughout and the other three were to drive at certain specified events. David Porter was to be honorary team manager and to handle the paperwork. In fact, Keith and Wendy only participated in speed trials and hill climbs and Richard did only three events.'

Jim, along with Mike, was a fan of the sport and, as he put it, 'We were all quite close in family terms and all had a shared interest in watching racing so it was just a natural progression.'

The fledgling team could have had a spectacular break if only they had realised it at the time. They settled, eventually, on a Cooper-BMC T52 Formula Junior car for a number of reasons, but price paid its part in its discussions, as well as the fact that the BMC engine was prepared by the BMC factory. They rejected, ironically in hindsight, a Lotus as they felt the cars were 'too brittle'. However, the chance they had to really succeed was lost when they chose not to use a Ford engine, and I quote Meikle's book here: 'The Ford unit was not supported by a factory. It was just thrown together by a chap called Duckworth with whom David had been at college.' That 'chap called Duckworth' was Keith Duckworth who, along with Mike Costin, produced one of the most successful engine companies of all time in Cosworth. Cosworth won 176 wins as an engine supplier during a long and successful Formula One career.

After plumping for the Cooper T52, Mike, his father and his father-in-law, his cousin Jim Meikle, cousin-in-law Keith Hamblin and the only non-family member, David Porter, visited Cooper's Surbiton base. They were met by Ian Burgess, who had a long association with Cooper as a driver (racing for them in the 1958 British Grand Prix), mechanic and driving instructor. By 1960, he was also involved at a junior management level. Meikle was not overly impressed by his sales technique however, wryly commenting: "It should be a very noisy car" as one of Burgess' key unique selling points! But they bought the car for £1250, of which the engine and gearbox were £250 each. (This is around £25,000 and around £5000 in today's money respectively).

The Coburn team soon learned the perils and pitfalls of racing before they had even turned a wheel. They were advised to have the car delivered in kit car form, thus saving money and also giving them exemption from purchase tax. CERT felt this was OK as they could prepare the car well by excellent attention to detail. However, the parts all came at various times and behind schedule, so the meticulous planning turned into a rush job. They were also promised chassis number 1 from the factory. When it arrived it was chassis number seven. The BMC engines kept dropping valves and were so short on power that they continually went back to the factory for development. Eventually, as Meikle describes, "Doug Johnson from Cooper phoned to say that 'Your box has quite a few bits in it now and you might as well come and take them away'."

Even then, CERT had a lot to learn. With no instruction sheet, assembly was carried out 'by guesswork, common sense, a memory of the chassis seen at Cooper and a small cutaway drawing from *The Motor.*' It is easy to be sniffy, looking back now, at CERT's somewhat naïve and amateurish efforts, but that shouldn't be the case. Putting together a racing car back then was no easy business with very little recourse and background information available. Apart from 'the box containing bits nobody knew what to do with', the construction went well. One of the rear wheels was out of line which entailed moving and rewelding the suspension mounting points, and the only other issue took a bit longer to come to light. In the first two races, the tyres were supplied differing front to back. Dunlop's racing representative noticed this at CERT's third meeting and Mike's comments that the car had 'impossible handling characteristics' soon vanished.

With a 1936 Eccles 4-berth caravan bought for £62 10s was to provide accommodation for the team. Some of the highlights listed by Meikle, which are worthy of repeating here, include 'an elegant china chamber pot' and, as Meikle enthuses, 'To have beds, a kitchen and a living

room with you in the paddock is luxury indeed. The rapidity with which plates of fried food emerged was only surpassed by the rate at which pieces of flaming toast followed the same route'. Much more importantly, a workshop being set up for CERT's racing division meant the team were pretty much ready to go. The workshop was basically a corner of the Coburn Engineers factory initially, with 'its own door and light'. Relative success led to a move to a larger but narrower workshop next door to the factory, with dedicated workbenches and racks and 'George the Welder' in the same workshop close by for any welding.

The team was almost ready for its first race. On 24 February 1960, the crew set off for Silverstone in Northamptonshire. They had to cope with both Porter's Alfa Romeo breaking down initially at Hindhead followed by their Commer Spacevan, which had the car and all the spares in, giving up the ghost at nearby Guildford with a broken exhaust. A quick transaction with Gray's of Guildford gave CERT a 5-tonne vehicle which saw them arrive at Silverstone at Midday. On a cold, wet day, Keith Hamblin and then Mike drove the Cooper round. The engine was, in Meikle's description, 'grossly inadequate'. The handling of the car caused a number of issues and then the gear locking plate broke and the lever had to be held by hand. One has to admire the resilience of the CERT team to keep on going despite all this trauma. It would have been far easier to just give up and go home.

Not least as the engine issues persisted. Again, Meikle describes the saga in such a colourful way, it's better to just quote him. 'With the first meeting less than two weeks away, BMC had not produced their latest engine, their best so far only developing 65bhp, which was hopeless. The management displayed a remarkable lack of interest in their customers, especially as their promised delivery was long overdue. John Cooper predicted an engine 'very soon'; Charles Cooper 'eight weeks'; Doug 'had to ring up about it', Ian Burgess 'why don't you have the old engine?' We had previously refused this but this was reluctantly agreed as the only alternative. The engine dropped in quite easily. While running the engine in the workshop, the wet felt used to muffle the noise from the exhaust pipe caught fire and the pipe glowed red hot. This was not one of our better ideas!'

With all the trials and tribulations behind them, it was finally time to go racing and the team turned up at the Goodwood Formula Junior race on 19 March. On a cold and damp day, Spence finished a very encouraging sixth in morning practice with a best lap of 1min 43sec. For comparison, John Surtees, in the Tyrrell Cooper, competing in his first four wheel race, was fastest in 1min 37sec. Spence had issues with chronic understeer and with his gearbox, but

Team CERT. From left to right: Malcolm Angood, David Porter, Mike Spence, Leo Ackroyd. *John Spence*

finished in sixth place after just missing out in a long duel with John Hine. Jim Clark won the race in his Lotus, with Surtees second, Trevor Taylor in the Lotus third, Peter Arundell in his Elva fourth. Three of those top four would become very significant in the Mike Spence story in due course.

A week later, Spence came fifth at Snetterton, with the biggest drama coming when a scrutineer took exception to the 'inadequacy' of Mike's crash helmet. Over the next few races, Mike and the team started to reap the rewards of some of their hard work. Mike was consistently up there with some of the leading drivers like Chris Threlfall, Peter Arundell and Mike McKee, but such was the closeness of the machinery that many drivers challenged for success.

Mike's first Formula Junior win came very early in the season, winning the MRC event at Snetterton on 21 May. On a pleasantly warm spring day, Mike was fastest in practice and was rarely troubled as he took the win and fastest lap. His nearest challenger, Mike McKee, broke a halfshaft on lap two and Mike was left to ease home some nine seconds ahead of Chris Andrews.

Mike followed this up with a second place at the next race which was the Cheshire Cup at Oulton Park before some three weeks later, taking another victory. His next win came at a place as far removed from Snetterton as could possibly be imagined – Monza in Italy. After travelling 750 miles, the team was met by extremely hot weather. Spence, whom the public address system insisted on pronouncing his name as 'Spenchy', recorded quick times in practice despite excessive valve bounce. In the first 15 lap heat, Mike won from Denny Hulme's Cooper and in the final itself, Mike was second behind Italian-based Briton Colin Davis in his OSCA, when a rod popped out of the side at Lesmo on the 23rd lap.

Mike took one more win that season, at Silverstone in September in the North Staffordshire Motor Club event, to round off a largely encouraging first season, with three wins and three second place finishes. Out of around twenty-two events, there were just three failures to finish which reflected on the sterling job CERT had done and Mike's consistency and mechanical sympathy, both of which would be reflected throughout his career. This was picked up by a number of people including journalist Paul Fearnley, who wrote in *Motor Sport* magazine many years later; "Spence was sensible, he did not crash and more often than not, finished in the top ten."

The 1967 Shell Motorsport Profile noted that Spence's results were even more impressive when analysed in context. Spence was in his own car and if that was written off, there was no works replacement or support. Although naturally always kind to his machinery, which was shown by his multiple finishes, it was observed that he still broke no end of

Mike racing at Oulton Park, 1960. *Ted Walker*

lap records and maybe if he had thrown caution to the wind, he would have won more races.

Meikle summarised the season in much the same vein in *All Set From a CERT*: 'The car never retired due to bad preparation and only had one mechanical failure (at Monza). Although, at the beginning of the season the Cooper was a world beater on paper, on the circuit it was anything but. The road-holding was inferior to the Lotus and Lola cars and the BMC engine seemed less powerful than the Ford. The aim for the team in this first season was to keep the car up to scratch in all respects. There is a lot to learn at the game and most of it can only be learned by experience. It was soon evident that it is necessary to take it seriously to be successful and that money is useful. The original idea of several drivers using the car during the season did not work out very well as to exploit a racing car to the full, constant practice is needed for the driver to be absolutely familiar with the car. Mike Spence drove the car well and set up new lap records at Snetterton, La Châtre and Silverstone. Proof progress was made was that on 8 April, Mike was reported by *Motor Sport* as 'another Cooper'. By the end of the year, it was 'the Cooper of Mike Spence challenging the established drivers for top honours.'

Mike seemed happy with the performance of the car when he took part in a little question-and-answer session with Meikle for the CERT publication in 1962: "When we first drove each Formula Junior car, we all thought it was fabulous. However, looking back, the old Cooper felt very hard, with big wheels and lots of unsprung weight. The car felt skittish at the back and also felt, at times, as if it was about to leave the ground. It oversteered of course, but it was very controllable, you could do pretty well anything with it."

At the end of the season, the CERT team sold the car for £850 to Ian Raby, who was later to compete in three Grand Prix races between 1963 and 1965. Now it was time for Mike and his band of merry men to take on a new and stimulating challenge.

Quick Emery

"It was noticed that the normal standard of workmanship at Emeryson was well below the level set and maintained by CERT. There are enough unpredictable risks in motor racing without adding predictable mechanical ones"

Jim Meikle, Mike Spence's cousin and mechanic

Mike passing Tim Parnell at Brands Hatch in October 1961 in his Emeryson Formula Junior car. *Harold Barker/John Spence*

At the end of 1960, Keith and Wendy Hamblin and then Richard Barneby decided not to be involved in the Formula Junior project any more, which effectively meant Mike and David Porter were on their own. They decided to carry on and Mike chose a somewhat risky option, as Jim Meikle put in *All Set From a CERT*: 'After considerable discussion Mike decided to buy a new Emeryson Formula Junior, an untried design not then completed or tested despite David's cries of Lotus, Lotus, Lotus, for reasons not disconnected with finance.'

There was a methodology behind the verdict to go for Emeryson. Coburn Engineers had a subsidiary company, which was called Peasmarsh Plastics. They made glassfibre bodies for the Emeryson team. This, in due course, helped smooth a transition to Mike joining the Emeryson outfit for the 1961 season as one of their works drivers.

The Emeryson team deserves a little background before proceeding further. Emeryson was run by Paul Emery, who was one of the two sons in the name of the outfit. Paul's father George was a car builder and Paul, and indeed his brother Peter, followed in the family tradition.

Emery was regarded as a brilliant engineer with ingenious ideas and excellent welding skills, but seemed never to have the financial acumen to take the marque further. In an extensive article in *Motor Sport* magazine in 1985, Emery recalled to author Mike Lawrence why he started racing: "I built my own cars because I wanted to race. But I never had enough money to go racing and to drive other people's cars. So the only way to race was to build my own car. When I progressed in Formula Three however, both as a driver and a builder, I couldn't afford the prices asked for an engine capable of winning, like a Norton for example, and so I packed it in as I couldn't compete against the Coopers." This was a particular shame as Paul had designed and assembled a fast and forward-thinking 500cc Formula Three car with front-wheel-drive.

Emery worked hard to achieve optimum weight distribution and to reduce weight. He also focussed on improving cooling with minimal air intake. As well as manufacturing the car, Paul built a 50 degree V twin engine which used two 250cc cylinders which significantly reduced vibration in the car. However, while it now achieved optimum lightness, the engine also achieved comprehensively intolerable levels of unreliability.

In vast contrast to the sport as it is today, it was somewhat more cost-effective for Paul to look at constructing a reasonably efficient Formula One car as opposed to a top Formula Three car, and as such Emery focused on developing his latest effort, with as Lawrence describes in his 1985 article, a more tubular chassis with an Alta engine which had differential mounted backwards with coil springs and a wishbone suspension to again increase air intake.

Emery even campaigned the car at the 1956 British Grand Prix at Silverstone, qualifying 23rd ahead of the likes of top sports car driver Umberto Maglioli, veteran grand prix driver Louis Rosier and future World Champion Jack Brabham in their Maserati cars. It was all for naught, as Emery made an early exit on lap twelve with ignition trouble. He made one more grand prix attempt himself as a driver but not in his car. He was in a Connaught Type B3 entered for the Monaco Grand Prix of 1958, which followed a decent result at the Aintree 200 a few weeks earlier. Emery, according to the Mike Lawrence article, said "That was the only time in my career that anyone ever gave *me* a drive". The entrant who gave Paul a chance? A man called Bernie Ecclestone, who later dabbled in Formula One a little bit...

By this time, Paul Emery had constructed a whole range of special single-seater and sports race coupés. But as Lawrence says in his *Motor Sport* article, Emery would never use a new part if a second-hand one would do. Money, or the lack of it, would consistently remain a problem until 1960, when another former grand prix driver, Alan Brown, became involved in the business. This allowed Emery a little more leeway to construct a number of lightweight Formula Two, Formula One and Formula Junior cars. It was into this epoch of the Emeryson era that Mike came along.

Before I refocus on Mike, it's best to conclude the Paul Emery story. He continued to be involved, to various levels, with the Equipe National Belge (ENB), Scirocco, Shannon and BRP-FPE Formula One projects until 1966, before he then became well known as a Hillman Imp tuner. As an aside, his has an amusing story behind it – according to Graham Rabagliati, who wrote in *Formula Junior Historic Racing Association* magazine, that it was the apparent speed of this new Emeryson, when driven by John Turner at the Montlhéry Formula Two race, that encouraged ENB to buy not just one but three Formula One Emerysons from Paul Emery. However, it was most probable that they did not realise that the impressive lap times were in part due to John Turner missing out the chicane on the majority of his laps! Emery's thinking was definitely innovative and some years ahead of others, he certainly would be as famous as one of Mike's later team principals, Colin Chapman, if Emery had the money (and maybe a bit of luck) to see the designs go one step further. He died in 1993, aged 76.

The new team was run by Alan Brown, with Paul Emery designing and constructing the car and Peter Emery the engine. Gordon Ross was the chief mechanic while a young teenage mechanic called Malcolm Angood joined later in the

Mike in the CERT run Emeryson Formula Junior car at Silverstone 1961, ahead of Bill Bradley's Cooper T56. *Michael E Ware/John Spence*

year. The idea was for the car to be a semi-works entry, but kept and maintained at the CERT workshop. The notion was that the car would have factory support and benefit from the latest modifications but in the event, this was not to be after the Emeryson factory ran into financial difficulty.

Bought for £900 (so therefore using all the money from Ian Raby for purchasing the 1960 CERT Cooper T52 Formula Junior car, plus £50 more), the car also had a Cosworth Ford engine this time (setting them back an additional £340), and a 4-speed Volkswagen gearbox. Mike chose the Cosworth over Peter Emery's dry sump version.

Jim Meikle was not impressed by the Emeryson set-up and wrote as much in the CERT book: 'It was pathetically inadequate for building and developing racing cars; with no cars in the shop, they were quiet and one made them impossibly busy. As the Ecurie National Belge were running a team of Formula One Emeryson cars and they crashed at least one per race, the workshop was busy and the progress on the junior car was slow. As usual, time was getting short and to get the thing finished, Mike and Leo Ackroyd, who was actually a watchmaker by trade and the tenant at what was a sort of gatekeeper's cottage at the entrance to the Spence family home at Coopers Bridge, spent most evenings working on the cars. This at least had the advantage that it ensured everything was assembled correctly and accurately, even though progress was hesitant, with much of the work being trial and error and involving endless arguments. It was noticed that the normal standard of workmanship there was

well below the level set and maintained by CERT. There are enough unpredictable risks in motor racing without adding predictable mechanical ones.'

Malcolm Angood, however, has fonder memories of Paul Emery: "Paul Emery was a dynamo. He was always on the go. He was quite a clever man but not quite as clever as Colin Chapman but, like Colin, Emery had lots of ideas. Paul was a nice chap and did not have a nasty bone in his body. Maybe that's why he did not quite succeed as he should have in the sport."

In the event, Mike's car was not ready until June. He was forced to miss the first couple of events and then drove Stan Hart's car as a works entry for another two meetings, with little to cheer when Peter Emery's dry sump engine either failed or proved problematic. Mike had another personal disappointment, when he was at the British Empire Trophy Meeting at Silverstone. Mike's idol and racing hero, Juan Manuel Fangio, was present and visited the grid, shaking hands only with the drivers on the front row. A frustrated Mike, who qualified seventh and was on the second row, could only watch on with envy. He went on to do well in the race, running in fourth before a gearbox problem put him back to ninth place, which was only his second finish all season to that point. The first had been at the preceding race, the Eastern Counties 100-mile race at Snetterton, where Mike finished in a distant 12th place.

It seems strange, certainly in modern-day context, that a Formula Junior driver with barely more than one year's single-seater racing experience could then make their Formula One debut, but that's exactly what Mike did at the non-championship Solitude Grand Prix, held at the Solitudering near Stuttgart.

Looking at it some sixty years on, it also seems unusual that Emeryson would focus on attempting a Formula One race, as opposed to giving it a miss and concentrating on correcting all the mechanical issues they were experiencing in Formula Junior. No matter; as it certainly did not do Mike any harm.

Mike continued to have trouble with the car in practice with the change of formula bringing no respite to his troubles. Initially he suffered from fuel starvation issues, due to the diameter unions being too small. This was soon rectified by Paul Emery using a portable drill. Emery then worked on the engine pick-up by modifying the accelerator pumps with a hacksaw. Later on in the first practice session, Mike lapped just three-fifths of a second slower than Stirling Moss in the UDT Lotus, who earlier that year had taken perhaps his greatest Formula One victory, the Monaco Grand Prix, ahead of the Ferrari duo of Richie Ginther and Phil Hill.

Eventually, once the final times were in, Mike was in 11th place out of seventeen starters, albeit only the first ten had been able to put down actual lap times in qualification. Mike's eleventh place was down to him having a faster lap in first practice than the other six drivers also unable to record a full practice time. He could possibly have done even better than that, be he had to finish practice earlier than planned when he ran wide at the twisty section of the track, ran up a bank and backwards into a straw bale leaning against a telegraph pole. A hasty rear suspension repair was undertaken by Paul Emery, Malcolm Angood and Gordon Ross.

Nonetheless, he was starting ahead of some notable drivers. Alongside him on the grid was wealthy and enthusiastic Dutch amateur, Carel Godin de Beaufort, who had ten Grands Prix to his name by then. The row behind him contained Wolfgang Seidel, a German driver who made his grand prix debut against the likes of Alberto Ascari, Mike Hawthorn and Juan Manuel Fangio in 1953, but also Maurice Trintignant, a veteran French racer with two grands prix victories – both at Monaco (1955 and 1958) – and a 1954 Le Mans 24-Hour win to his name.

However, in the Frenchman's defence, Maurice was now driving an uncompetitive Cooper-Maserati entered by the Scuderia Serenissima team, but to out-qualify – in whatever form – a man of Trintignant's calibre would have surely been a fillip for Mike.

At the race itself, Mike not only impressed, but he also had to overcome a major obstacle when the gearlever came loose and he had to hold it in place to avoid retiring. He dazzled in

Mike in his racing overalls. *John Spence*

a car significantly down in horsepower as he and de Beaufort battled for 11th place, swapping positions in the opening lap before Mike inched ahead. After seven laps, though, the gearbox finally cried enough. Innes Ireland won the race for Lotus, just a fraction ahead of the two Porsches of Jo Bonnier and Dan Gurney in what Jim Meikle described as 'one of the most exciting races in years'.

One of Mike's most notable Formula Junior performances, and certainly one of his most significant wins in this fledgling stage of his career, was the Commander Yorke Trophy 100 mile race held at Silverstone on 29 July 1961, which also gave Paul Emery a massive amount of credit as a constructor. This was just days after Mike's Formula One debut at Solitude and perhaps some of the momentum and adrenaline from a good performance there continued to seep through.

Enjoying the benefit of a good start, on a dry and fine day, Mike led early on from Philip Robinson in his Alexis and Geoff Breakell's Lotus. Breakell took the lead on lap six but Spence remained on his tail with Robinson close behind, as the trio circulated around the club circuit at a consistent lightning pace. The pace proved too much for some, including future grand prix driver David Prophet, whose car overheated on the 13th lap. Robinson, Breakell, Mike and Jack Pearce (also in the Lotus) continued to stay ahead of the chasing pack at the 50 lap mark. Mike, who was in fourth place with 25 laps to go, seized his chance five laps later when Robinson spun, ironically somewhat as he was now in control of the race for the first time, with Breakell having to take avoiding action to avoid the stricken Alexis. Spence took full advantage and then with the benefit of a clear track pulled out a string of fastest laps to take an ultimately comfortable win, by 15 seconds, ahead of Breakell. It was not Mike's first Formula Junior win but by piloting the Emeryson to victory over the Lotus cars was a noticeable achievement.

Graham Rabagliati, in his article for the *Formula Junior Historic Racing Association* magazine, found a summary of the race from the BRSCC newsletter that gives a flavour of the race: "The main event was the Commander Yorke Trophy race, which resulted in a thoroughly deserved victory for Mike Spence in his works entered Ford-engined Emeryson. Spence, who had achieved fastest lap in practice, duelled for much of the race with Geoff Breakell's Lotus 20 and the Alexis driven by Philip Robinson. These three were engaged in a fierce struggle, often passing the pits side by side in a manner reminiscent of Baghetti, Bonnier and Gurney at the recent French Grand Prix".

Unfortunately, apart from this win and the Solitude race, there was little to really celebrate in 1961. Mike's career certainly seemed to have, by and large, gone backwards. At least the latter end of the season saw more finishes with a

Mike racing in the British Empire Trophy, Silverstone, 8 July 1961. *Ted Walker*

couple of sixth place finishes at the BARC Formula Junior Championship race at Silverstone, a sixth and ninth place at Crystal Palace's September Trophy and then another sixth and ninth at the BRDC Clubman's double-header at Silverstone.

Mike appeared at another F1 race, a national event at Brands Hatch where he finished second to Tony Marsh – a result even more impressive when considered that Mike had no clutch or brakes on the last lap after hydraulic fluid failed on both systems. Meikle again could not hide his frustration with the season as whole: 'The Emeryson was handicapped from the beginning by being a brand new car that was never really developed. The season was spent much more on building than developing. Although it was powered by a Ford engine, it was only of 1000cc capacity, whilst everyone else was taking advantage of the extra power produced by the 1100cc powered cars. The handling, although superior to the old Cooper, was never entirely satisfactory.

'The results for the year were therefore not inspiring, but were certainly commendable when the extent of the strength of factory opposition is considered. Special credit must go to Leo Ackroyd and Malcolm Angood, who together worked long hours and, due to whose considerable efforts, what could well have been a complete debacle was transformed into a reliable racing car.'

Mike gave his own thoughts on the car to Jim Meikle in the CERT book: "The Emeryson was considerably softer than the Cooper – a big improvement. But when on the limit, it always gave me the impression that is was on the verge of control – which was very nasty. It oversteered on the fast and medium corners and understeered on slow ones."

Happily for Mike, things would soon take an upward turn with an association that would remain with him to his dying day.

Mike at the John Davy Trophy, 1 October 1961. *Ted Walker*

Lotus Blooming

"Mike Spence was very smooth and completely relaxed and this to me was quite outstanding. I knew then that with experience he would develop into a really first-rate driver"
Colin Chapman

Malcolm Angood and Leo Ackroyd pose over Mike's Lotus 22 in the Ian Walker colours. *Mike Spence/Lynne Spence*

In the early stages of 1962, Mike decided that he would commit to motor racing full-time, giving up his engineering role at Coburn. He spoke to his father and uncle who supported him and were enthusiastic about his chosen career. Again, his father repeated the mantra to Mike that he first uttered four years previously when Mike wanted to start racing: "What you must do, you must do".

As Mike recalled to both Peter Miller for *Men at the Wheel* in 1963 and Bill Gavin for *Autosport* in 1965, 'I had realised that I was doing a lot better than I had anticipated. When I found out that it was relatively easy for me to do well, I decided to make racing my career.'

With every respect to the CERT outfit, Mike was still involved with an amateur organisation. No matter how good Malcolm Angood was as a mechanic and how competent and well-meaning the likes of Meikle, Angood, Porter and Ackroyd were, it was clear for Mike to make the quantum leap upwards, he would need either an affiliation or a piece of luck.

In the end, Mike got both pieces of the jigsaw at the same time. Enter Ian Walker. Unlike some of the other names that appear in this book whom were an integral part of Mike's progress from Formula Junior to Formula One, I am not going to expand too much on Ian Walker, as much of his life and career is covered in the brilliant book *Ian Walker Racing – The Man and His Cars* by Julian Balme. But for those who do not have Balme's lavish tome, Ian Walker (1926 to 2008) was a charismatic, fiercely loyal, incredibly professional and supportive team manager. Initially, Walker was a driver himself, initially in rallying and then, most memorably in sports cars. He was a long-time friend of Colin Chapman, having met the Team Lotus founder during his sports car days.

Walker ran a racing team, on and off, for much of the 1960's with real success at various disciplines. The likes of Mike, Graham Hill, Paul Hawkins, Frank Gardner and Jim Clark raced his cars, with Ian using his links with Chapman to great effect to secure an official affiliation with the works Lotus team.

Ian Walker Racing was founded in 1962. The epiphany came at a test held at Goodwood in January 1962, which was supposed to tie up Walker's single-seater plans as a driver. Instead, as he confirmed to Balme, his plans changed and he retired there and then from competitive driving; "I found myself watching other drivers and thought they were good. Wouldn't it be fun to be instrumental in their respective careers, I wondered to myself. I noticed Mike, among others, that day. I was impressed by his verve and style."

Business and family pressures had also put an end to Walker's driving career, but he got involved with his new

Mike Spence and Ian Walker. *Julian Balme*

direction with great gusto. Mike had already bought a Lotus 22 to compete in, somewhat caving in to pressure from David Porter that the only way to progress in Formula Junior was driving a Lotus, even if CERT ran it themselves, but Walker agreed a deal with Mike where the latter would also drive the team's Lotus 23. Ian would pay for spares and do all necessary paperwork. Mike, for his side of the bargain would maintain and transport the car, subsequently receiving 20 percent of any start and prize money, plus bonuses. Mike had actually initially bought a Cooper and put down a £100 deposit, but as the car was not ready for the promised delivery date, there was no option for a trial run, so he switched to the Lotus 22 before Walker intervened.

Jim Meikle mentions in the *All Set From a CERT* book that this agreement went very well for both men: 'This turned out to be a very satisfactory arrangement. Mike could always be trusted to finish in the first four places and by the end of the season had taken well over £2000 in prize, start and bonus money.'

Although Mike and his team had established a workshop in Berkshire, it was Ian Walker who, in many ways, transformed it. Walker's mantra was to cut the cloth and save as much as possible, however what was bought, at the best possible price of course, would be the best quality available. Walker insisted on the car being painted a distinctive hue, choosing a shade of yellow akin to English mustard. Ever an astute businessman, he knew that the car would stand out for fans and potential sponsors. Spence himself followed this lead and painted his helmet with virtually the same colour scheme, choosing a rather garish mustard yellow (Meikle describes it as 'bilious') to stand out from the other drivers in the team. This started a trend and was partly why Mike went through a number of distinctive helmet designs in his career, all of which were eye-catching.

Chapter 4

Despite Walker's commercial nous, feelings were mixed as to his overall influence and legacy on Mike's season. Malcolm Angood, the team's mechanic, had a slightly unsentimental view on the team owner: "Ian Walker was OK, but he was more of a businessman. Quite a hard individual. But we did not really work with Ian as closely as we did – as it were – with Paul Emery. Ian entered the cars but it was the CERT team that did all the work, set-up and so on. We did not see him a lot of the time and were left to our own devices."

The combination of the Lotus 22, the hard work of the CERT team members and Mike's mechanically-sympathetic and consistent performances led to a string of excellent finishes to start the season off in a positive manner. It was not until the tenth race of Mike's season that he failed to finish and, even then, this was not a mechanical failure as Mike was caught up in a crash on lap nine of the 30-lap final of the Gran Premio della Lotteria when in fourth place. Before that, there were two successive second place finishes at the Anerley Trophy heat and then the subsequent final at Crystal Palace, impressing many onlookers from the Formula One paddock with his speed, overtaking and fairness in a race-long battle with Alan Rees. This event was the support race to the Formula One non-championship event that weekend. Mike would recall at the end of the 1962 season that, in his career, it had been his toughest race thus far: "The hardest I've ever had to race is at Crystal Palace, albeit it's not much of a circuit, in that battle with Alan Rees."

He also came in second place in the prestigious Monaco Formula Junior race, splitting the two official Team Lotus cars of (winner) Peter Arundell and Bob Anderson. While he may have picked up a few admirers from his Crystal Palace exploits, Spence's future was already pre-destined in the stars as a result of an eagle-eyed observer at the Monaco event.

New Zealand journalist Bill Gavin recalled in an article in *Autosport* magazine about Mike in 1965 that he was left amazed by Chapman's thoughts about Spence and how

Mike standing in front of the Ian Walker transporter. *Julian Balme*

highly Chapman rated him: 'In 1962, I was discussing Formula Junior drivers with Colin when he surprised me by declaring the most promising of his Formula Junior drivers to be Mike Spence. At that time, I considered Colin's high opinion a trifle unusual. Three years on, I asked him just how he had assessed Mike's now obvious ability so early.

'Colin replied, "At Monaco in 1962, I watched the Formula Junior race from a balcony of the Hotel de Paris overlooking the left-hander into Casino Square and the following right-hander. From there, I could see a driver's every movement in the cockpit – the way he turned into a corner, slid the car and every minute correction he made. I was struck by Mike's very good natural style. Of course, Pete Arundell won that race and Pete is a first rate driver. But from up there, I could see that Pete was fighting his car every inch of the way. Mike, on the other hand, was very smooth and completely relaxed and this to me was quite outstanding. I knew then that with experience he would develop into a really first rate driver. You might say that we started grooming him for stardom from that day".'

Despite the two higher profile races recorded above, Mike's finest moment at Ian Walker Racing came at the

Mike, with a yellow helmet in Ian Walker's yellow liveried Lotus 22. *John Spence*

David Porter stands over Leo Ackroyd who is working on Mike's Lotus 22.
Mike Spence/Lynne Spence

Alan Rees leads Mike Spence and Denny Hulme in the Anerley Trophy, 11 June 1962. *Julian Balme*

most desperate time for the team when he won the Coupe Internationale de Vitesse des Juniors at Reims. However, this win would not have been possible had Mike's mechanic, Malcolm Angood, not noticed there were broken valve springs under the rocker box cover in the engine after qualifying. He changed them and, in doing so, helped towards Mike reaching a top speed of 144mph on the fast straights that Reims was famous for.

Julian Balme praises Angood as a mechanical master in the Ian Walker book for his assistance but, true to form, Malcolm saw it in a practical way: "Regarding Reims? Well, it was just natural, there was certainly no mechanical wizardry! It was just the sequence of things. You did compression checks and sometimes you would find faults and you would then work on rectifying them. The engines were not complicated at all; they were Ford four-cylinder engines so that was quite straightforward. What I do remember is whenever we went to races like Reims, all the local garages would stop servicing local cars and open their garages up to racing teams, so each of us would have a local garage to take the car back and look at it properly and that definitely helped, even more so in this case."

Mike drove, as referred to by Doug Nye in his *Story of Lotus* book, 'A dogged race. It was a smooth, consistent performance which marked him down as a man to watch and many took note.'

However, unbeknown to Mike, the fast nature of the circuit would cause terrible tragedy for Ian Walker and the team. Mike's team-mate was Pete Ryan, a young, courageous, blisteringly fast and skilful Canadian of American heritage. His father helped establish the Mont Tremblant circuit in

Canada. Ryan was beginning to make a real name for himself due to the above attributes, but on lap five of the first heat, a thrilling battle between Ryan, Peter Arundell (Lotus), Frank Gardner (Brabham), John Love (Cooper) and Bill Moss in his Gemini, culminated in Moss and Ryan touching wheels and cartwheeling off the circuit at the fast right-hander Gueux turn. Moss only had minor injuries, Ryan succumbed to his a few hours later, dying aged just 22. A potential star of 1960s motor racing was gone before he could realise his potential.

Mike, when prompted by Jim Meikle at the end of 1962, skirted somewhat around the issue of accidents. "You don't usually have time to think to yourself during a race about whether a nut has been tightened, but on a circuit with a long straight like Reims, it might occasionally occur to you as you see the wheels flapping up and down. Accidents don't really affect my driving, even when I see and hear them, no I don't think so. In a race, you have to concentrate too much to think about it. You may worry about it very much before the start, but during the race, there's no time."

Mike overcame initial – and consistent – wheel balance and handling issues in the early part of the season to become a contender for race wins. He was often up at the sharp end of the grid in practice and towards the front in the race. In his very first race for Ian Walker, at Snetterton in April 1962, Mike even led a couple of laps before his rear brakes locked and he spun. Even then, Mike came through the field to take sixth place from a lowly 15th. In all, he took eight second-place finishes, including the aforementioned meetings at Monaco, Monza and Crystal Palace, but also at Albi (twice) and then at the slightly less exotic races of the London Trophy (also at Crystal Palace) and the Vanwall Trophy at Snetterton.

There were four third place finishes as well, including an early morale boosting fillip at Goodwood's Chichester Cup but also took third in the John Davy Trophy and perhaps most spectacularly of all, coming from 23rd on the grid to finish on the podium at the second heat of the Grand Prix de l'ACF at Rouen. There were two fourth place finishes and then another five finishes in the top seven that season.

Fuel starvation, broken valve springs and selector forks caused some consternation too, but Mike finished the majority of races in what Meikle describes as 'A busy year but a satisfactory one, Mike probably being the most successful driver of any privately entered Formula Junior car'. Normally, this kind of consistency might have even warranted a title challenge, but Peter Arundell was in a class of his own that year, winning 12 races, way ahead of Alan Rees on four.

Meikle rounds up the year's issues mechanically: 'Not being a factory entry, detailed knowledge of the settings required for the car were not readily available and had to be found out by sifting the rumours, then trial and error. Such things as wet weather settings, braking ratios, gear ratios and suspension settings now played a very important part in the game. The main troubles recurring with the car involved the clutch and gearbox. To reduce the risk of the clutch failing, it was adjusted as far back as possible, with the result that as soon as it got too hot, it did not work. This possibly aggravated the other trouble with the gear selector forks which seemed to be particularly acute.'

Malcolm Angood pushes Mike's car at the 1962 Formula Junior race at Monaco. Jeremy Cottrell watches on in his Cooper T56-BMC car (94).
Ted Langton-Adams/Vince Howlett

Malcolm Angood: "The Lotus 22 was a good car, a nice car. Never broke, nothing silly went on with it. As long as it was prepared properly, it always went well."

Although biased, Jim Meikle in his book *All Set From a CERT*, is probably right in his assessment of Mike's career over the last few seasons. 'Mike's results have always been extremely satisfactory. During the three years, only three incidents can be recalled – a partial spin at Brands Hatch, the trip into the woods at Monza with the Lotus 22 when attempting to lap a backmarker and the spin into the bank at Solitude in his first outing in a Formula One car. This is a remarkable record.'

John Pledger, one of Ian Walker's most trusted mechanics and Walker's effective right-hand man, noticed something about the young driver that helped his progress. He recalled to Paul Fearnley in an interview for *Motor Sport* magazine that 'Mike was very quiet. There was none of the buggering about that team-mates Frank Gardner and Paul Hawkins got up to. He was a very serious, focused young man.'

Ian Walker may have taken a back seat when it came to preparing the car, but where he really came into his own was when it came to opportunities to progress or to seal a deal. He was very instrumental in Spence getting the Team Lotus drive due to his contacts with Lotus and Colin Chapman. Chapman was already impressed with Spence's driving, but Walker certainly would have had the nous to work a deal out that would work for Mike as well as himself. Mike bought a Lotus 27 car, after Colin Chapman offered him good terms that he sometimes made for promising drivers.

Malcolm Angood, Mike Spence and Ian Walker before the start of the Formula Junior race at Monaco, 1962. Mike's race performance was spotted by Colin Chapman and led onto great things for the future.
Ted Langton-Adams/Vince Howlett

John Fenning (56) in his Lotus 20 leads Mike and Richard Attwood as they lap Martin Gould (64) at the BARC 200 Formula Junior Race at Aintree, 1962.

Julian Balme

Mike's successful 1962 season had allowed him real credit and helped with money thanks to the race results deal agreed with Ian Walker at the start of the season. Further funds came Mike's way as he was able to sell his Lotus 22 (to Ian Raby again) for £1100.

It was now time for the band of brothers from CERT to go their separate ways. Leo Ackroyd, who made the engagement ring that Mike presented to Lynne, remained with Ian Walker for a few years. He remained in the UK until 1977 before the onset of ill-health prompted a move back to his native New Zealand, where he passed away a short while afterwards. Jim Meikle stayed in the publishing world and is still alive, residing in Devon. Jim recalled to me from his home there "After Mike moved up to Formula Two full-time, I did not see him as much and his career developed from there. We would not have guessed how well he would have gone on to do, but he had chosen to race professionally and take it seriously and we knew he would do his best accordingly. Although we were family and somewhat biased, we knew that he was a pretty good driver by his performances." David Porter became Mike's business partner and *de facto* manager. He later moved to Zimbabwe to work for Tate and Lyle. He died in the early 2010s.

Malcolm Angood later worked at Ron Harris Team Lotus and briefly at Mike's workshop before leaving to set up his own service and repair business in Soho Mills, Woburn Green, which is near Bourne End in Buckinghamshire. He specialised in Lotus cars and a lot of former Mike Spence staff ended up working with Malcolm. He was also mechanic to famed hillclimber David Good and briefly raced himself.

"When I raced, I learnt from Mike. You're with someone all the time so you do pick things up. We worked together for many years. When at Coburn, Mike and I were supposed to be working on sliding doors all the time, but we would often be building Mini rear-engined cars instead. He always had that mechanical background. Racing was his passion and we would work in the evenings and every weekend on that Mini and so many other projects. It was a good time."

More recently, Malcolm, who also raced powerboats, ran a business that manufactured radio frequency interference shields, optical lenses and glasses and optical mirrors. Malcolm was seriously ill with cancer for a while before I started writing this book, but it is testament to the strength of his friendship and his fondness of Mike that he managed to speak to me for around an hour while in terrible pain. I got the feeling he would have liked to have talked for longer if he had the strength to do so, but I knew deep down that our hour-long chat on a warm summer's night may well be the only one we would have. Sadly, I was proved right. On his 78th birthday, on 29 November 2020, Malcolm passed away with wife Diana by his side.

For Mike, now formally seconded to the Lotus junior ranks with a three-year contract and a career in ascendency, it meant a move to the squad endorsed by Chapman to run their official works Formula Junior cars which was the Ron Harris Team Lotus outfit, where he joined Peter Arundell and John Fenning.

I won't introduce Ron Harris too much as I'll let those who knew him explain more about the man, but to just give a tiny background not in the below, Harris bought two Lotus

20 cars for John Gee-Turner and Mike Ledbrook to drive in Formula Junior in 1961. He impressed a number of people by the way he ran his team and remained involved with the sport until an unsuccessful and stressful foray to Argentina in the early 1970s. He died on 18 September 1975.

John Fenning takes up the memories of Ron Harris in detail: "Ron was an ex-motorcyclist who took part at the Isle of Man TT, so he was not a bad racer. But he really made his fortune through developing 16mm films and made a lot of business by renting these out to prisons and the armed forces and so on. He did very well and as far as I was concerned, he was a pretty wealthy guy.

"After World War Two, he wanted to do motorcycle racing again but not as a racer, so he entered John Hogan, of BSA Bantam fame [Hogan rode and tuned the BSA Bantam, which was a two-stroke lightweight motorcycle that was produced by the Birmingham Small Arms Company] before moving into car racing when Formula Junior came along.

"My break came in 1961 at Brands Hatch in a Lotus 18. I'd come in fourth place in practice in a national race meeting so we were delighted, it was a really good result. My father and I were by the car and the trailer and we were astonished to see Peter Arundell coming towards the car and taking a look. We had a quick chat and he said, 'Bloody quick today boy, well done,' and went off again. Well, we were astonished with that, but before we had time to think about it, another man, a stockier and older man came across to the car. It was John Hogan, to which I replied '*The* BMA Bantam John Hogan?'

I couldn't believe it! Anyway, John was working for Ron, who had told him to come and find me and offer me a test drive in a Lotus 20. We went from there before becoming a works driver for them."

"Well, I was to be the number Two driver because he already had John Gee-Turner as his number one. However, at Oulton Park, Gee-Turner had a tank-slapper of an accident and ended up the wrong way up – in the water! He was married and was soon persuaded to pretty much retire on the spot, so I became number one and number two with two cars to drive!

"We were very lucky with the Lotus 20s in 1962. They were a year old, of course, but in the winter of 1961 to 1962, the regulations changed that the engine capacity went up from 1000cc to 1100cc which was an extra 20kg. Cosworth developed a new engine around that time and the extra engine power that gave us was significantly better and overcame the handicap of the extra weight. A good engine makes all the difference. We were now extremely competitive and in the first few races we were right up at the sharp end.

"Half-way through the 1962 season, Harris was approached by Eric Broadley of Lola to run the Lola Formula Two team, and John Hine joined me and then Colin Chapman approached Ron to become the effective Lotus works Formula Two and Formula Junior team in 1963. Mike and Peter Arundell joined me. So that's how the Lotus link-up came about. Ron told me I would be driving but I had no idea it would be the monocoque car.

Peter Arundell leads Mike Spence at Snetterton, 1962. *Julian Balme*

"Ron Harris hated only two things with a passion. He hated flying and he hated the dentist. He had somewhat funny teeth because he couldn't stand dentists! He was a bit of a Marmite character. Some loved him, some couldn't stand him and sometimes I think it was mutual. I liked him, but he had some quirks. He wore glasses with very thick lenses, which was fine, except when he was driving! He would zoom off at over 100mph or more, but his eyesight just couldn't react properly to those speeds and it was a frightening experience!"

Malcolm Angood, who joined Mike at the team: "Ron Harris was a nice chap. He was not in our face, he let you get on with it, took it all in. If we needed him, he would be involved, but otherwise he left it to the team to sort and he would enter the cars. He gave us a lot of trust, a really lovely bloke. No trouble at all, he rarely poked his nose in or caused a problem. He was certainly *au fait* with motorsport through his motorcycling though."

John Fenning remembers the Monaco Formula Junior race in 1963 very well as a personal disaster for Harris in particular. "Ron would always have his notebook and work out maximum prize winnings and how much profit he would make once he took all other expenses out of the equation. I remember that because we were doing well that year, he had worked out what would happen if we finished 1-2-3.

"So, in qualifying, I was approaching Casino Square and I brushed ever so slightly, minutely, against the kerb, but I lost control of the car, slid into the Armco at Casino Square and the steering arm was completely bent, so I was out of the qualifying and the race. I was full of doom and gloom for obvious reasons and was about to walk back when along came Mike, who lost it almost in the same place as I did and hit the straw bales on the other side of Casino Square. I was

Malcolm Angood, Ian Walker and Mike Spence before a Formula Junior race at Brands Hatch. Note Mike's trainers compared to racing boots. The man in the bobble hat with his back to the camera is John Cooper, the legendary constructor and co-founder of Cooper Cars. The driver in car 43 is John Love who was racing for Ken Tyrrell's Tyrrell Racing Organisation. Despite the coats, this is from the John Davy Trophy on 6 August! *Julian Balme*

so relieved that I was no longer the only dickhead to crash that day! So I was walking back on one side of the track and Mike on the other. I caught his eye and we met up and walked down to tell – as Mike called it – the good news to Ron that both his cars were out and he was down to one car. Poor Ron. Peter Arundell was left, qualified and then retired on the first lap with a broken crankshaft. Ron's profit margin for his potential 1-2-3 was completely ruined!"

Fenning also remembers Mike well, but got on a whole lot better with Peter Arundell: "We all got on very well and very quickly. There was no nastiness between us, no pushing or trying to look better for Ron and Colin. Peter and I were both motor mechanics by trade and so we got on like a house on fire as we had a shared interest. Mike, on the other hand, was very reserved and very shy; my wife remembers him as quite painfully shy. Quite quiet, a little aloof, or that's what I thought at the time. He would never join in anything social that we would do. I mean, me and Peter used to arm wrestle! Mike would never join in anything like that. I often offered to drive him to race meetings because we weren't too far away from each other but he always preferred to make his own way there and rocked up by himself."

John Fenning is now in his early 80s. A real enthusiast of the sport, he competed for many years in historic single-seaters. In addition to this, he owned and operated a motor

Leo Ackroyd, David Porter and Malcolm Angood share a joke at Goodwood but Mike doesn't... unless he's wiping tears of laughter from his eyes!
John Spence

racing seatbelt company. He briefly raced in Formula Two, but injuries from a road car accident somewhat curtailed his single-seater career, but his business was taking off anyway.

Going back to Mike, his first race for 1963 in the Lotus 27 with the Ron Harris team was scheduled to be the BARC Spring National race at Oulton Park, but the car was not ready in time. Eleven days later, he had a car – but only just – for the Chichester Cup at Goodwood. It was pretty much out of the box and there was no opportunity to develop it or even take part in practice. Mike started 21st and finished eighth. Ninth place at the International Trophy at Silverstone, the crash at Monaco as mentioned above and then an early suspension failure at the Anerley Trophy at Crystal Palace, scene of one of his better drives a year before, meant it was a slow start to the season for Mike.

It was in France that he started to pick up consistent results. He finished fourth at both Rouen and Reims, and a strong second, on aggregate, at the Charade circuit in Saint-Genès-Champanelle near Clermont-Ferrand. No doubt buoyed by this, he also finished a strong fourth at the British Grand Prix support meeting at Silverstone. But thereafter his luck ran out.

Gearbox failure accounted for his race at Solitude after just three laps, whereas flywheel problems were the reason for retirement at Zolder. A broken transmission ruled him out of Goodwood and being caught up in a multi-car collision at

Zandvoort on the very first lap continued a moribund set of results. The first year of his Lotus multi-year contract was not going all that well.

Mike certainly did not appear to be on the cusp of greatness, or even the cusp of Formula One, unlike his team mate Arundell who was winning all and sundry that season. It was noticeable to some just how unremarkable Mike's results were.

Bill Gavin covered Mike in some detail in an article in *Autosport* in 1965, but one of the initial paragraphs was quite blunt: 'His recent victory at the Race of Champions was the culmination in the ever-increasing form he has demonstrated since replacing Arundell. His current success in Formula One baffles many who were unimpressed by Mike's performances during four years of Formula Junior Racing'.

Competitor Richard Attwood, winner of the 1963 Formula Junior race at Monaco, was also slightly surprised. "I was amazed that he drove a grand prix car as early as 1963 and that Colin Chapman had taken a shine to him when he saw him driving in the 1962 Formula Junior race. I also remember that he was pressured into making that mistake in Casino Square in 1963! Mike Spence was a fairly quiet sort of guy, shy and quite difficult to assess. In Formula Junior days he was just another driver trying to make it. But when you are doing what you are doing, little else distracts you, and I had hardly any idea what Mike was doing at the time."

Mike in the Lotus 22 at Brands Hatch, 1962. *E Selwyn-Smith/John Spence*

Leo Ackroyd and Malcolm Angood with Mike's Lotus 22.

Mike Spence/Lynne Spence

Other competitors at the time remember Mike positively as a person, but more as an equal as a driver. Certainly it appears that Mike was regarded as a good driver, but not one whose performances really stood out. When his competitors talked to me about his races in Formula One or sports cars, they could remember a race, or a manoeuvre that particularly impressed them. Those I spoke to about Mike in Formula Junior struggled to recollect any similar notable moments in 1963 although, to be fair, it is hard to recollect every race that you might have competed in, let alone what someone else did or did not do nearly 60 years earlier.

David Hobbs, outrageously underused in Formula One, with just seven races in seven years between 1967 and 1974, enjoyed a very long career in sports cars, with a Le Mans class win and a Trans-Am title to his name. But back in the early 1960s, he was a competitor of Mike's and they mingled through the next few years before Mike's death. "In 1963, I drove in Formula Junior and it was quite a big thing in those days in terms of judging a young driver's form. I drove in Formula Junior for Midland Racing Partnership and Mike was driving for Team Lotus in Formula Junior. Mike's goal was to race in Formula One and my goal was to do the same!"

"Really, the only team we were thinking about was Lotus. He had a bit of a head start as he was driving for Lotus, but I'd spoken to Colin Chapman because I'd raced the Elite the year before that very successfully so I had some connection with Lotus. In the championship, that year, I had a couple of great races. At Silverstone, when I came second to Denny Hulme by two hundredths of a second, and then I came second in my first race at Oulton Park to Peter Arundell, who had beaten Mike – and everyone else – in the Formula Junior.

"Towards the end of the year, it was getting a bit nip and tuck in terms of placings in the series, but in the last race at Brands Hatch I managed to crash in practice, which Colin Chapman did not seem to think much of and that more or less put the kibosh on it. Mike later ended up being a driver

Mike and John Fenning go back to the pits to tell Ron Harris the good news that two of the three Ron Harris entries are out in qualification! *John Fenning*

for Lotus in Formula One, which at the time I would have loved to have had, but obviously now, with 20/20 hindsight and bearing in mind what happened to Mike and a whole bunch of other Formula One people, it doesn't really matter that I did not get to Formula One with Lotus."

"Mike and I used to get on reasonably well. We would bump into each other in various races. He was a little bit ahead of me in Formula Junior as he pretty much started in single-seaters where as I drove in a Morris or a Jag or whatever we had at the house. He drove proper racing cars right from the word go. But there was not much in it and Arundell was the class of the field"

Alan Rees (who later drove in Formula One and became one of the founders of the Arrows Formula One team): "He was certainly a good driver and our level of performance was quite similar so we had lots of good races against each other. He seemed to be quite a quiet and reserved person."

Even some of Mike's key supporters felt progress was slower than hoped. Colin Chapman, for one, also shared some of

Gavin's doubts when discussing Mike in the same article above: 'It has taken him a little longer than even I thought it would to really get cracking on with his career.'

So it was pretty clear that Peter Arundell was set for better things and Mike needed a bit of luck and confidence to reboot his Formula Junior career. But as fate often has its twisted way of turning out, it would be Mike who would make his grand prix debut in Italy one week after the Zandvoort start-line debacle and not Arundell.

Spence's debut came about because at the Mediterranean Grand Prix at Enna, held around Lake Pergusa, current Lotus Grand Prix driver Trevor Taylor was fighting for second place with Lorenzo Bandini when the Italian driver went wide. It sent dust and stones right into Taylor's path. He lost control and hit the banking at 140mph. Taylor was thrown out and suffered heavy bruising but nothing more serious. The car was destroyed even before it subsequently caught fire. Trevor Taylor was not fit to drive at Monza, so normally this would give Arundell his debut. However, Arundell was concentrating on Formula Junior commitments. Mike was to drive the same

A relaxed Mike on the grid in his Ron Harris Lotus. *John Spence*

car, the Lotus 25 R3, that Jim Clark had competed in at the non-championship event at Karlskoga one month before.

The 1963 Italian Grand Prix, which was Ferrari's 100th World Championship grand prix (if you exclude the private entry at the 1950 French Grand Prix), is now best remembered as the race where Jim Clark took his first World Championship title by winning the race. In doing so, he became the first driver to win a World Championship with three races of the season still to run, such was his domination that year. Lotus also won the Constructors' Championship, the first of seven they would end up winning. It was also the last World Championship Formula One race held over 300 miles, with the organisers initially choosing to use the concrete banked track as well as the race circuit.

The warm, dry and sunny weekend did not start well for Mike. The car developed a few minor problems so he did not have the opportunity to practice on the Friday afternoon session to become accustomed to both the car and the extended track. His fortune soon turned when Bob Anderson lost a wheel when driving on the south banking when his rear-stub axle sheared off after hitting a bump.

This gave the banking naysayers an opportunity. The police went around and decided that the organisers had not provided sufficient spectator protection around the insides of the banking. They pronounced that they would not sanction further use of the banking for racing. Mike therefore only had to concentrate on the road circuit, which he knew reasonably well, but he still progressed no further as problems with both cars (Jim Clark suffered a gear mechanism failure) meant Friday saw no laps completed at all.

On the Saturday, Mike was in the old Lotus 25 and instantly impressed. He turned a lap of 1min 40.9sec in the older car, which esteemed *Motor Sport* journalist Denis Jenkinson described as 'praiseworthy'. He was just 3.6sec off pole-sitter John Surtees in his Ferrari, but had also out-qualified former grand prix winners Innes Ireland (now in the BRP-BRM but a former winner for Lotus), Jo Bonnier, Phil Hill, Maurice Trintignant and Giancarlo Baghetti and had come close to matching former World Champion Jack Brabham.

Race day saw Mike drive a consistent and largely unspectacular race but, helped by other retirements, he had moved within sight of the last points-scoring place of sixth, just holding off the Cooper of Tony Maggs for seventh place, when his oil pressure started to fall on lap 73. Mike could have carried on but realised the engine would be destroyed if he did so, once again showing signs of mechanical sympathy, he pulled to the side of the circuit and stopped. Maggs would go on to take sixth place. It marked the side of Spence which David Porter remarked on about his friend: "Mike would never go beyond his own limits if he could and never push a car beyond its limits if it was not safe to do so." While this race was the start of many bright and blossoming developments for Mike, it also saw the abrupt end of one element of Mike's racing career that he had sustained since his debut in single-seaters.

Peter Procter, Mike's long-time competitor in Formula Junior and Formula Two takes up the initial story. "I remember him, personally, as a nice guy, who was a little quiet, but one whom you could always have a chat with. But the one thing I particularly remembered about him is that he would drive in plimsolls. Not even special plimsolls, just the normal trainers. I never found out why, maybe he thought they would help him grip better. But nobody else ever wore plimsolls, we all wore normal racing boots!"

Cedric Selzer was Jim Clark's mechanic at the time and there was only one thing he truly remembered about Mike: "He only drove in one grand prix while I was at Team Lotus. I remember that he turned up and drove in plimsolls which caused a great deal of merriment in the team". What Colin Chapman said when he eyed the plimsolls is lost for eternity

but sure enough, Spence did not wear them again for a grand prix after that!

The grand prix debut marked a high point in a rather mixed season. Mike summarised his thoughts to Jim Meikle at the end of the season: "The Lotus was the only one of the three cars I drove in Formula Junior to have enough power so that the inbuilt understeer could be properly used. When I got to know the car, and when being really pushed, I always felt fully in control of the car, rather than vice versa. It was much more comfortable than the other cars, but the cockpit was hot. It was definitely at its best on a fast circuit, with fast open corners. Formula Junior has changed quite a lot. Cars have developed and speeds have increased and the whole thing has become more important. It will, of course, be called Formula Two in 1964. It undoubtedly is more competitive and is now taken more seriously by the various teams who participate. The series and the racing is less like a game and much more like a job of work."

Mike was not to know it, but he soon would get much more grand prix experience in 1964 than he could have expected.

The start of the 1963 Preis von Tirol. *John Spence*

1964:
Opportunity Knocks

"I was trapped underneath and fuel was flooding everywhere. I was completely trapped. I lay there listening to everything ticking away. I had to yell at the marshals to put their cigarettes out"
Mike Spence

Mike puts on his helmet before the race. *Peter Darley*

ike was to remain at Ron Harris Team Lotus for 1964 but now in the new Formula Two championship, which replaced Formula Junior and attracted a number of the current grand prix drivers including Jim Clark, Jack Brabham, Tony Maggs and Graham Hill. As Doug Nye opines in volume 3 of his BRM opus, *The Saga of British Racing Motors*, 'Formula Two really became special as world-class superstars were racing against young new hopefuls wheel-to-wheel; what a wonderful schooling.'

Alan Rees, one of the class of 1964, concurs: "When Formula Two started in 1964, many of the top Formula One drivers competed in this formula such as Jim Clark, Jack Brabham and Jackie Stewart. This was really exciting for young drivers like me coming into the formula as they could really gauge their progress against the top drivers, and so too, of course could the top teams."

Colin Chapman attempted to produce a new chassis that could run in production for both Formula Junior and Formula Two that covered the technical regulations for both seasons. The Lotus 27 was the result. It was the first monocoque car for junior formulae and it was narrow, five inches slimmer than its predecessor, the Lotus 22. The chassis was more up to date and revolutionary but only cost £65 more to build.

However, Mike was destined to never race the Lotus 27 in Formula Two, instead competing in vastly improved machinery compared to what he had driven before as he was in the Lotus 32. Chapman had developed the 32 especially for lower formulae, with this car having a 997cc Cosworth engine. The Lotus 27 then became the Formula Junior car for 1963.

Part of the reason for the switch, overall, to the Lotus 32 was because the Ron Harris team struggled initially. The winter of 1963 and 1964 was bitterly cold and early pre-season testing was snowed off. The Lotus 27 was therefore undeveloped much more than its competitors. The chassis, with glassfibre outer skins was not rigid enough so Colin Chapman had to revert to aluminium panelling; only then did they start to do well. But Chapman, ever the innovator, was never one to stand still and the Lotus 32 soon came into development.

So far in Mike's story, it's been relatively straightforward – by and large, it was one team and/or one car, whether it be the CERT Cooper T52 in 1960, the Emeryson in 1961, the Lotus 22 run by Ian Walker in 1962 or the Lotus 27 with Ron Harris in 1963. The 1964 season would see the first variable year for Mike as he appeared in a number of different cars, albeit all of them being of Lotus origin. If I were to try and write about Mike's season chronologically, it might get a bit bogged down in criss-crossed detail, so instead Spence's 1964

Mike in the Ron Harris Lotus at the Formula 2 race at Aintree, 1964.
Peter Darley

season is split up into different sections based on which Lotus division he ended up driving for.

Let's focus on Formula Two with Ron Harris first of all. All in all, he drove twelve races in Formula Two with the stable that season. He won his class in the first race of the season, the non-championship Aintree 200. He finished sixth in the overall race, no mean feat in itself. One week later, he took an impressive third at the Eifelrennen round. His next race, however, the London Trophy at Crystal Palace was anything but stellar as an engine failure on the very first lap led to a swift exit.

Engine failure would continue to blight his Formula Two challenge, with another two failures at the Vanwall Trophy at Snetterton and the GP d'Albi. But he took a third place at Reims and then, best of all, he won his heat at the Autodromo di Pergusa circuit in Sicily, winning after 20 laps. Nonetheless, at the end of the year, Mike was crowned *Autocar* Formula Two champion, which ended up being the only championship Mike ever won.

It is important, however, to put that title into context. That championship was only open to British and Commonwealth drivers on the results of all national, national open and international F2 events of not less than 24 miles held in Britain, a whole surfeit of caveats there. Be that as it may, someone has to win and Mike, largely on the strength of his performance at Aintree, took the title from four points ahead of Tony Maggs' Lola-Cosworth.

One of the secrets to Mike's success was his smoothness, his natural relaxed driving style. Mike himself said to Jim Meikle that the drivers he respected the most were similar to him "I look for relaxation, smoothness and rhythm in a good driver. They are fast, but they don't look fast." Jim Meikle, in my conversation with him in 2020, offered a little bit more insight into Mike's way of racing. "Mike took after his father in so many ways. They were both always good at golf and tennis and, of course, Mike did well at cricket, all things that require hand-eye co-ordination. They seemed to be born with that natural ability that some people have. Mike obviously

Chapter 5

Mike at the Nürburgring. *Günther Kever/archive Nils Ruwisch*

Mike smiles for the camera. *Peter Darley*

developed it over time, but that sense of balance and co-ordination was always there. I loved being driven around by Mike in whichever road car he was driving. He always drove in a very relaxed and smooth way but was fast with it. I remember being driven by Jim Clark once when we went to a race in Germany and he was the same, a very good road car driver. They both had that natural ability that I did not have and others don't have."

Mike would race with Ron Harris again in 1965 (and briefly in 1966), but more of that later. The next team to enter Mike's racing career were The Chequered Flag, run by Graham Warner. Like Ian Walker, Warner was affiliated with Lotus and also like Walker, has had his life profiled by in a book; this one by Richard Heseltine in 2013. If Walker's background briefly needs filling in Mike's story, so too should Graham Warner's own tale be summarised.

Warner established a sports car showroom in Chiswick High Road in 1956. Two years later, he hit onto the idea that he would enter motorsport with members of his sales team driving to improve their car prowess and sales technique. Helped no end by public relations expert John Webb, later to become long-time circuit manager of Brands Hatch, Warner's business became well known very quickly. So much so, that a parts manager at Lotus Components offered to help set up any Lotus car Warner ran if he could drive for them. That parts manager was Graham Hill, later to become a World Champion and Indianapolis 500 winner, and a true legend of the sport.

Chequered Flag then became the Lotus distributor for the London area, but they also constructed a single-seater car, the Gemini, to try and meet demand for the fledgling Formula Junior championship. In essence, things snowballed from there, with Warner giving Jim Clark his very first single-seater drive at Brands Hatch on Boxing Day, 1959. Warner would then go onto enjoy great success in GTs, Formula Junior (Charlie Kolb won the Sebring International Formula Junior

race in 1961 in a Gemini beating illustrious opposition) and Formula Three (running the Brabham works team) before spells in Formula Two (running the McLaren works team) and briefly in Formula One (running a Brabham BT42 for long-time protégé Ian Ashley in 1974).

Mike first came across Graham in 1963. Colin Chapman was receiving many enquiries regarding a Lotus Elan racing car. He sent his two development drivers, Mike and Peter Arundell, to help tweak the car at a test at Goodwood. Spence helped suggest developments, improving the car's grip and weight distribution. Then, in 1964, Chapman decided to have both Ian Walker Racing and The Chequered Flag team run a Lotus 26R Elan in sports car events. The former had Jim Clark, Peter Arundell and Trevor Taylor, whereas Warner would have Mike and a young Scot who was also in Formula Three, one Jackie Stewart.

Spence drove in selected races when available. He had planned to compete in more events for Warner but fate would decree otherwise, which will be explained further on in this chapter. Nonetheless, Mike drove in the 15-lap Sussex Trophy at Goodwood, enjoying a race-long battle for a class win versus Peter Arundell, missing out by just 0.4sec. Spence also drove in the Guards Trophy at Brands Hatch, finishing second to team-mate Stewart, before winning the 2.0 Litre GT Tourist Trophy race at Goodwood, winning by a comfortable 13.2sec in what ended up being the last race that the Chequered Flag team entered a Lotus Elan. For completion, Mike also raced at Mallory Park for Warner's outfit, finishing in fourth place.

The third man in Mike's racing life in 1964 was Alan Mann, for whom Mike also raced with in 1968. In 1964, though, Mann was involved in the Ford Cortina Lotus programme in the United States, and Mike had two rather low-key races for his outfit at Pensacola and Laguna Seca in the Cortina, of which I will delve into more detail shortly. The race at Pensacola's Corry Field, a US Naval Station, was previewed by the *Pensacola News Journal*'s sports editor Al Padgett, who featured on Mike in his column. He was warm in his coverage of Mike, picking up on his relatively rapid rise from starting racing to being a works Lotus driver. "He's no Graham Hill, but Graham Hill was no Graham Hill after four years of racing," Padgett correctly surmises.

Alan Mann (1936 to 2012) was an occasional racing driver who ran a number of Ford cars in saloon car racing in 1962, initially under the name of Andrews Garage and the name was tweaked to Alan Andrews Racing in 1963, when he prepared a Ford Cortina GT for Henry Taylor, a former grand prix driver who later became Ford's competitions manager. Taylor and Mann linked up at the Marlboro 12-Hour race in 1963, did very well indeed and impressed John Holman of Holman and Moody, one of Ford's works teams at the time. For 1964, Mann, with his now eponymous outfit, became a Ford factory team in rallying and sports cars and, over the next few seasons, the team won a number of races and titles, including the 1967 and 1968 British Saloon Car Championship with Australian driver Frank Gardner. Mann reignited the team in 2004 and, despite his death, the team still continues in historic racing to this day.

Peter Procter remembers him well. "Alan Mann was very straight. I only knew two honest people in motor racing. One was Alan Mann and the other was Ken Tyrrell. I never had a contract with Alan Mann, everything was done with handshakes. He would give me a bundle of money as I was owed. A very honest and a very generous man. He was such a nice chap, a real gentleman and very intelligent.

"His general prep of cars was brilliant. Very rarely did one of his cars break down. What a lot of people forget is that Alan was a very quick driver himself who would never think twice about taking the car out to give it a go. You felt confident in one of Alan's cars. That's why I did so well in the Tour de France rally, as you had the confidence to push more. The cars handled extremely well. Alan Mann oversaw

everything personally. The preparation, the organisation, the accommodation and everything was always done *so* well. Unfortunately, though, Alan never had the backing, even with Ford help, to have done even more in the sport."

Spence returned to the Ian Walker Racing Team fold for one more drive in 1964, although the original plan was actually for two races – the first to be the Nürburgring 1000km, the second the Le Mans 24-hour endurance event.

It only ever turned out to be less than one lap. Before he even started his quick lap, Mike crashed at over 150mph, one of the worst of his career. The coupé overturned and slid for around 150ft, utterly destroying the bonnet. The car was a total write off, but Mike thankfully survived unscathed.

Gordon Horn, one of the team mechanics, recalled to Julian Balme for Balme's Ian Walker Racing book about the crash: 'Mike reckoned the pedal went hard, but not to the floor. My theory was that the engine, being rubber mounted, had moved forward, trapping the brake pipe as it ran from side to side along the rear of the cross member. Of course, the car was such a mess after the accident, it was hard to tell.'

Mike's memories of the crash were recalled to Bill Gavin of *Autosport* one year on from the crash: "The car climbed a bank, went through the fence and rolled. I did not have any idea where it finished up. I was trapped underneath it and the full load of 38 gallons of fuel was flooding everywhere because the filler had broken open. I was completely trapped. I couldn't even move to turn off the ignition and I just lay there listening to everything ticking away. When some marshals did appear, they were smoking cigarettes, so I had to yell to them to put their cigarettes out."

Finally, before I come back to the main focus of Mike's 1964 season, let's return to the Ford Cortina programme. In 1962, Ford of Britain approached Lotus with the idea of fitting the Twin-Cam engine, designed by an engineer called Harry Mundy, into one of their production saloons and building one thousand of them to qualify for Group 2 homologation. This was duly achieved in September 1963.

Mike in the Chequered Flag entered Lotus Elan in the Sussex Trophy race at Goodwood, March 1964. **Peter Darley**

The wrecked Ian Walker entered Lotus Elan at the Nürburgring 1000km race which Mike was lucky to survive. **Nils Ruwisch archive**

Chapter 5

This had mainly occurred because Colin Chapman had yearned to build his own engines for Lotus, largely because of the cost of the Coventry-Climax engine. The choice of which car to build lay between the Ford Anglia and the Cortina, and the latter was chosen for its more upmarket appeal. Lotus would work on chassis and suspension and Cosworth, led by former Lotus designer Mike Costin, would concentrate on developing the engine.

The Ford Cortina had instant success, finishing ahead of the previously dominant 3.8-litre Jaguars on its debut at the 1963 Oulton Park Gold Cup. Soon Ford was running cars in Britain, Europe, and the USA, with Team Lotus campaigning cars in Britain for Ford, and Alan Mann Racing running cars in Europe, also on behalf of Ford.

Team Lotus actually had to split itself up somewhat into four divisions to concentrate on all the extra work. Team Lotus concentrated on Formula One, Team Lotus Racing with Ford of Britain focused on the British touring cars, Team Lotus Racing with Ford of America worked on the Indianapolis 500 and sports cars in America, and Team Lotus Racing with English Ford Line (Dearborn) concentrated, with Alan Mann, on the touring cars in America. In addition, there were official works teams in lower formulae like Ron Harris and Ian Walker Racing.

The Cortina is well remembered by those who saw it in action, with an almost signature move around any bend of the inside front wheel off the tarmac and in the air due to a set-up of soft rear suspension and a hard front end. There are many photographs of Jim Clark perfecting this technique, but Jackie Stewart and Mike Beckwith also enjoyed success.

Mike only raced a Ford Cortina sporadically but it was such an iconic car of its time that many involved with Mike in the Lotus programme at that time remember it very fondly.

Peter Procter: "The Ford Cortina was head and shoulders over anything else. People like Sir John Whitmore just drove

away into the distance. It was very, very well prepared and handled *so* well. They used to make quite a thing about Jim Clark lifting the Cortina on two wheels. Well, everyone who raced it did! I've got loads of photos in my home doing the same thing. When the Cortina entered those fast corners, they had such good handling that the lift was natural.

"I can only remember one retirement, which was at Snetterton, and that was down to a relatively minor thing. Otherwise, they ran like a dream. I remember when I did the Tour de France, which was thousands and thousands of miles across France's public roads, it never once missed a beat. It was just fantastic."

Mike's luck with the Ford Cortina was not as good as Procter's. Indeed, at Oulton Park, a burst tyre pitched the Cortina into a barrel roll on lap 13 at the Esso Bend. Thankfully, Mike emerged with no injuries bar a few bruises and scratches.

Jackie Stewart was also not quite so keen on the Cortina: "The Lotus Cortina was the most difficult car I had ever driven in my entire career, it was a ridiculous car. But it was fast! Jimmy, John Whitmore, Jack Sears and I went fast."

Bob Dance is one of motorsport's unsung heroes. He became Team Lotus mechanic in 1960 and still, at the age of over 85, is working at the Classic Team Lotus historic car preparation and restoration based in Hethel in Norfolk. He worked for Lotus from 1960 to 1969 and then again from 1977 until the team disbanded in 1994. Ten years later, he joined Classic Team Lotus. Bob is a modest, humble and quiet man, but with an unabated enthusiasm for the sport and when, in my long conversations with him researching the book, his enthusiasm and encyclopaedia-like knowledge of the Cortina programme was evident by the upbeat tone in his voice.

Bob recalled: "The Cortina team was set up with Team Lotus and Ford, but was set up in America. Now we started building the Cortina in Cheshunt but it needed 1000 cars built so it could be homologated a touring car which kept us quite busy to say the least!

"What we used to do was keep the same mechanic on each of the three Cortina cars we had for consistency. In 1964, we had Peter Arundell, Jim Clark, Jackie Stewart, Mike Spence and John Whitmore. Bob Davies was Mike's mechanic at Roskilde and Bob Sparshott for the rest of 1964. Roy Parsons went over in the States to work for English Fordline with Ford because it needed a dedicated person over there."

To finish the brief part the Ford Cortina played in Mike's life, one of the key memories David Hobbs had of Mike (and it is a significant and insightful one) was from a touring car race at the Roskilde circuit in Denmark. "In 1964, I had to make a critical decision as my dad's company that I worked

Mike (car 31) and Jack Sears (car 30) lead the pack at the 1965 BRDC International Trophy race at Silverstone in their Lotus Cortinas. *Peter Darley*

Mike smiles in his Ford Lotus Cortina. *Peter Darley*

Bob Dance (left) and Mike Spence. *Peter Darley*

for, a transmissions company, went belly up. Me and my wife – we had one little kid and one on the way at that time – had a big heart-to-heart. Should I turn professional or should I go back to what I did before? I'd been an apprentice for five years with Jaguar. I was a bit of a half-hearted engineer and had not done well in my exams as I was so busy racing. Anyway, Lotus contacted me. It was a chap called Andrew Ferguson, and he asked if I'd be interested in driving a Lotus Cortina in a handful of races. The first one was to be in a place called Roskilde, which is no longer there, it is now a housing estate in Denmark.

"Mike and I both went over there and drove Cortinas. We had a good time there. It was a two-heat race and I won the first heat from Mike – that did not go down very well. I think Mike thought that as he was an established Lotus driver that he should have won it. Anyway, he won the second race. Then we had a very funny evening with Bob Dance. I can't remember much of it, but Bob will!"

Bob Dance chuckled for a while when I mentioned this race which makes me suspect he knows more than he then admitted: "Well, if there was anything really dramatic, I would remember it! I did not drink *that* much, honest! I do remember going to that circuit though. Back then, the Cortina team was well funded by Ford. We had swish transporters. I drove it from Cheshunt to Roskilde. We went through Germany, then from Rostock to Gedser and then to the circuit. The circuit was only a mile round and it was very basic.

"As I say, I can't remember what David might be talking about, but I do remember we got up to a lot of mischief when we went abroad. One year, I think it was in France, we took the stand that holds all the flags before the start of the grand prix. We used to collect our own types of souvenirs and trophies and brought them back. The trouble was when we [Lotus] moved to Norfolk, we had nowhere to put them!

You must remember that, although things were different then, we would not always be with the drivers, especially with the Cortina team. Often we'd be given the names of who would be racing and it would not be the same person for every race. It might even be a different person for every race."

Back to David Hobbs: "Then I drove the Cortina twice more in the States, but Mike did not come over to those races and he then was probably doing some Formula One for Lotus. Well, Mike got mad at me for winning that race at Roskilde."

Hobbs' recollection of Mike seems to be one of the few examples that Spence outwardly took defeat badly. The almost universal recollection of Mike is that of a thoroughly equable, composed man and driver. However, before anyone dismisses Hobbs' recollection because it runs against the norm, Mike's mechanic for that race, Bob Sparshott, not only confirmed Mike's annoyance but revealed why he might have felt differently about that race compared to others. "Yep, I remember Roskilde with David and Mike. Now, both were very worried about this new upstart called Jackie Stewart! Both saw him as a threat for their respective futures at Lotus. Although we had a good time there, that might be why Mike was a bit upset that day."

But all of the above, even Formula Two, was largely secondary to the biggest change in Mike's career in 1964 and it revolves around a man whose name appears frequently in this book: Peter Arundell.

Arguably, although it was not planned, Arundell had more influence on Mike's career path than almost anybody. Just how good Arundell was – and could have been – is somewhat forgotten now. He died in 2009, aged 75 with a low-key response by the motoring press, by and large. Mike Lawrence wrote extensively about Peter in an article in *Motor Sport* in 1984 and that forms the basis of an effective pit-stop to talk about Mike's team-mate and rival.

Peter Arundell. *Peter Darley*

Peter Arundell speaks to Colin Chapman in his Ford Cortina. *Peter Darley*

John Fenning, Mike Spence and Peter Arundell, Monaco Formula Junior race, 1963. *John Fenning*

Peter Arundell speaks to his mechanics, including Bob Dance (right).
Peter Darley

Not all smooth sailing for Peter. Sid Carr (partially obscured) tries to fix Peter's car at Brands Hatch. **Peter Darley**

Unlike Mike, Peter Arundell did not have a boyhood fascination with racing. His interest came in a slightly unusual route, when tinkering with an Austin Seven while serving in the RAF, he happened to come across a feature in *Motor Sport* magazine about someone else building, racing and winning in an Austin Seven. That 'someone' was Colin Chapman!

But it would be about six years before Peter started to properly take part in competitions with his modified MG. A win over Tim Parnell in a sports car race at Mallory Park was the trigger for a change of focus and he bought a Lotus Eleven, which he prepared himself. In 1959, he impressed Colin Chapman when he consistently challenged Alan Stacey in the works Lotus. A few false starts occurred before they agreed a deal as Arundell recalled to Mike Lawrence, 'Colin said he'd still like me to drive for him – if I bought a car. I had no money so we agreed he would lend me a car, which would be entered by Team Lotus, though I was to prepare it and pay for spares and at the end of the season, I would sell it and pay him the purchase price with interest. Part of the deal was that I had to drive to team orders and I was the recognised third man behind Jimmy Clark and Trevor Taylor. That was frustrating because I reckoned that, in equal cars, I could beat Jimmy and would beat Trevor, but, driving to orders, you can never be sure.

The 1960 Formula Junior season saw Arundell finish no lower than fourth in a race, and he also took three sports car wins in a Gilby-Climax. But he was getting frustrated with Chapman as he told Mike Lawrence.

"Colin had almost a love affair going with Jimmy. He spent the bulk of his time with him, had a few words for Trevor and me he almost completely ignored. I was getting pretty cheesed off about it. As we sat on the grid for the last race of the year, at Brands Hatch, he talked to both Jimmy and Trevor but did not come near me. It seemed that I might be out of a drive for 1961. That got to me and I decided to

forget team orders and win, so I did. Trevor's gearbox went on the line and I beat Jimmy fair and square. I then had to sell my car to pay back Colin and, advertised as the 'Clark beater', it made me a fair profit. Colin was not amused by that, but he got his own back.'

Nothing changed immediately. In 1961, he was now only number two to Trevor Taylor with Clark now in Formula One. Peter still had to prepare the car himself, but Lotus gave him spares. "By this time, there were Formula Junior races going on all over the place and Trevor and I would often go off to separate meetings, both of us winning on the same day. Consequently, I began to get quite well known on the Continent, though less so here. The fact that Trevor and I had to drive to orders did not affect us off the track, we got on very well together, but it was still frustrating. Then came a race at Silverstone which was run in two heats with times deciding the final placings. Colin was not there, Trevor and I were in separate heats, and Mike Costin whispered in my ear. We both won our heats but I won overall, 15sec clear of Trevor."

Arundell bided his time and did his best and in 1962, blitzing the opposition in Formula Junior. From 26 races, he took 18 wins, 12 of them in internationally, one being the coveted Monaco Formula Junior event, his second successive win there. Arundell started to progress to Formula One at the same time as Mike Spence. At the end of 1963, he was entered for two non-championship Formula One races at Solitude and Enna and came second in both in his Lotus 25. "I felt I'd been ready for Formula One for some time, so I did not feel overawed. Chapman later told me that, because I'd beaten Jimmy in that last race at Brands Hatch in 1960, I'd had to do an extra year in Formula Junior, as a punishment. That apart, we were actually getting along quite well, though with Jimmy in the team, it was pretty well a one-car outfit."

For 1964, Arundell therefore joined Clark in both the F1 team and in the works Lotus Cortinas, with an additional

Formula Two programme in Ron Harris's team. "Again, we were driving to order, I felt there were times I might have beaten Jimmy in the Cortinas but we were not even allowed to mix it a little to put on a show."

Arundell impressed immensely in Formula One. At Snetterton, in the first race of the year (non-championship), Peter led in the wet after qualifying third before a broken transmission failed. He harried Clark at Goodwood at the second non-championship event of the season before finishing third, which is the same position he then finished at in Syracuse, Aintree and the International Trophy at Silverstone.

It was also third place that Arundell took in his first World Championship event at Monaco. He qualified sixth and may have finished higher than third but for transmission problems. He was third yet again at Zandvoort for the Dutch Grand Prix and fourth at the French Grand Prix to lie in a strong fourth place in the World Championship in his debut season.

Then came Reims, in a Formula Two race where Arundell was badly hurt in an accident. "I couldn't remember anything about it for years, but now it's mostly come back. I was in a tight slip-streaming bunch, you could be first one lap and seventh the next, when I kept my eye in the mirror for a fraction too long, got onto the rough at the kink on the straight, corrected, slowed slightly and was hit by poor Richie Ginther.

Jochen Rindt later said I went fifty yards in the air, over the level of the trees. I parted company with the car at the top of its climb and landed on my head and shoulder, while the car landed on all four wheels, relatively undamaged. I might have been OK had I been wearing seat belts but, on the other hand, my weight might have caused the car to land the other way up."

Peter Procter raced in that fateful race and remembered the incident well: "The crash was his fault. When I saw him again after he returned in early 1966, he asked me if I remembered anything. Well, I was right behind him and saw everything. It was his fault as Arundell put two wheels on the grass and lost control, going back onto the circuit in front of all the cars. But I did not like to say this to him because it had been such an effort for him to return, I felt it might impact that somewhat."

Alan Rees was also in the pack behind Arundell and Ginther as the crash occurred. "He had a bad accident in the Formula Two race at Reims in 1964, from which I felt that he never really recovered. He tangled with Richie Ginther in that race which resulted in his accident. I also had an incident with Richie Ginther in the same race before Peter had his accident. Ginther had placed his offside wheels inside the line of my wheels on the straight when I was right on the edge of the circuit and had nowhere to go. Fortunately we didn't touch, even though we were doing about 140mph at the time."

Mike on a damp track at the Solitude Grand Prix, 1964. *Etienne Bourguignon*

Despite the rain, it was a swelteringly hot meeting. Mike and Jim Clark strip off to cool down. *Etienne Bourguignon*

Arundell's right femur had snapped and he was in a coma for over a fortnight with his wife, Rikki, by his bed and 'Jabby' Crombac, the English-speaking reporter for the French magazine *Sport Auto*, also there to give her support and to help translate the medical feedback. The operation to repair the leg should have been straightforward, but while inserting a Steinmann pin to hold the fracture, the hospital (which Peter describes as 'squalid') inserted an infection as well. He was walking on crutches in a month and should have been fit for 1965 but surviving French medicine was more difficult than surviving a near-fatal accident. Osteomyelitis set in and, for over a year in England, he was in and out of hospital and in plaster and leg irons. He also shed three stone in weight.

Chapman had promised to keep a drive for him, if he was fit enough, and he was as good as his word with Arundell returning some 15 months later. The Chapman/Arundell relationship may never have been close, but Colin had Peter in his team for seven years. Arundell says, "If he had realised how much I worshipped him, things might have been different between us." The fact is, though, when a designer has a genius driving for him, the number two almost always is neglected. At Brands Hatch on 29 November 1965, Arundell stepped into a Lotus Formula Two car and finished the day within a second of the lap record. "I was pleased, knowing things would improve, but had I told them the truth about my fitness, they would not have let me near a car. I was not only worried about having lost my touch but, because I was a professional driver, about being out of a job."

Alan Rees: "I got to know Peter well when he was a team-mate of mine in the Formula Junior Lotus Team. We travelled to all the European races together and socialised quite a lot. Peter was probably the dominant driver in Formula Junior

Fully dressed, Clark and Spence converse before the Solitude Grand Prix. *Etienne Bourguignon*

before it was replaced by Formula Two in 1964. He was a very consistent and professional driver. Peter continued to race when he recovered, but he never quite got back to his old form. Within two or three years, as far as I remember, he retired and went to live in Florida with his German wife. At that point, I lost touch with him".

John Fenning: "If Peter was ever frustrated or angry with what had happened, he never said anything or showed it outwardly. It was a bit of a different era so you would not always do that sort of thing, but we were very much kindred spirits. He was bloody quick."

Bob Sparshott: "Peter was very much in Jimmy Clark's shadow. He always knew Jimmy was quicker. He used to come in, ask how fast Jimmy had gone. Peter then aimed for that time but then Jimmy moved the goalposts with a quicker time. I think Pete found it very frustrating. Mike did not worry about all that, he was very laid back. He knew his place. That said, at the time Mike died, he could have gone on to achieve major things as he was very good. Peter was not as nice as Mike, he was more hard-nosed and more arrogant."

With Arundell very much at his ascendency, one man's misfortune is another man's gain. But according to Peter Procter, Mike was not the only option to replace Arundell: "Colin Chapman was interested in me but always said I was not hungry enough. I never chased a drive but because I had the building business, I did not concentrate on it full-time, as I did not want to push it too far. Maybe that was the difference between me and Mike. He never chased a drive either, but he did have that little bit more hunger to make it a career. Colin kind of looked down at me and dismissed me in his mind for not being hungry enough."

The decision to replace Arundell with Mike seemed quite straightforward as he was a Lotus junior driver with at least some experience of grand prix racing. He had also shown enough promise in lower formulae to warrant at least a few races to show his ability. Of course, a chance to drive in the reigning constructor's champions number two seat would have been of interest to many, but joining a team so geared around its leader would also have been viewed as a poisoned chalice. Mike was fractionally ahead of David Hobbs, as Hobbs admitted above, whereas John Fenning's Lotus works career was starting to enter its decline. Pedro Rodriguez had driven for Team Lotus for two grand prix in 1963 but was not part of their works squad and had more North American experience than European at the time.

But there were plenty of drivers with experience without a grand prix drive at the time of Arundell's accident. Tony Maggs, with 21 races and three podium finishes behind him did not have a drive for 1964 after leaving Cooper. Masten Gregory, who also had three podiums to his name, enjoyed a top-line career stretching back into the mid 1950's but was also out of grand prix racing in 1964. The wild but fast Willy Mairesse was no longer at Ferrari and, in Formula One terms, was effectively a free agent.

In spite of their availability though, Mairesse's reputation as a car breaker would not have worked with Team Lotus, and Gregory had a solid drive with Ford in sports cars. It is also doubtful he would have taken up the number two position at that point in his career. In retrospect, Maggs would have seemed a perfect fit. He was available, fast and experienced. But Colin Chapman had invested a lot into junior teams. The production line manufactured promising new drivers to drive their grand prix cars, so naturally he wanted a return on his investment. Spence was, therefore, the natural choice for the role.

The first race Mike had for Lotus after Arundell's crash at Reims in 1964 was the British Grand Prix at Brands Hatch in the R8 on 11 July. Mike recalled to Bill Gavin in an *Autosport* article in 1965, that he was advised to keep things simple: "I was under strict instructions not to bend it, do not overdo

Mike seems very nervous in the next few shots at the German Grand Prix, 1964. Here he is lost in his thoughts on the grid at the Nürburgring.
Jack Fooshee/Walter Fooshee

anything. I was told to finish, so I toured around and came in about ninth but suffered with fuel starvation at the end. It was one of those odd days that no-one seemed to drop out." There was another reason for Chapman's caution. The Lotus 33 was, at that point, very new and had only been raced once up to that point. Although Mike and Jim Clark practiced in the new cars, they elected to race in the Lotus 25.

Mike was in the Lotus 25 for some of the 1964 season. The Lotus 25 was a revolutionary monocoque car. The first monocoque racing car appeared in 1912, with the name coming from the Greek 'monos' and the Latin 'coccum', meaning single-shell. The car was a single-shell structure, similar to an eggshell. The Lotus 25 changed motorsport, as the multi-tubular space frame chassis was replaced by a stressed-slim fuselage. It largely beat all opposition in Clark's hands, albeit only when it survived to the end.

A week later, at the non-championship Solitude Grand Prix, Mike was in second place, behind only Clark, when a steering arm broke. "Thankfully," said Mike to Bill Gavin, "because of the rain, I was not actually going that fast when it broke." This grand prix was the first race that Mike chose to wear a new helmet, one which he would become synonymous with – a red flamed or phoenix-like design at the front of the helmet with an orange-yellow tinted area at the back. He kept it a surprise for the race; during practice he had worn the bright yellow one that he had worn since the Ian Walker days.

Malcolm Angood: "I always thought I knew about the helmet, but maybe not! I always thought it was when he went over to Chaparral. A chaparral is a bird [a road runner] and it was supposed to be the kind of a tuft of a chaparral. He had it sculptured and airbrushed. It was all the rage in America at

A somewhat pensive looking Mike before the Solitude Grand Prix, 1964.

Etienne Bourguignon

Mike in the Lotus 33 at the 1964 German Grand Prix. *Etienne Bourguignon*

that time to have helmets like it, airbrushed with some kind of image or fiery-looking image. I can only presume he saw something or someone when he raced a Ford Cortina in America."

After his races in Britain and Germany, the next outing was the Mediterranean Grand Prix at Pergusa. Mike set the fastest race lap on his way to fifth place and the speed of the circuit was shown when Mike's quickest lap was the fastest single lap in Europe, achieving an average of 141.86mph in his Lotus 25.

In contrast, the very first World Championship Austrian Grand Prix, held one week after Pergusa, was not a great success for Mike. Former Lotus mechanic Arthur Birchall narrates the story of this Grand Prix from the team's viewpoint: "My first encounter, I think, with Mike was at Zeltweg, for the Austrian Grand Prix, in 1964. He was in the Lotus 33, which was not in the top ten of my favourite cars. The car was not that strong and the circuit was very bumpy. It was not long before Mike was in the pits during practice

A rather concerned Mike at the 1964 German Grand Prix with Derek Wilde beside him. *Etienne Bourguignon*

with gear selection problems. We made some attempt to repair a bent chassis member that was touching the gear linkage. This was a start line special and early on the chassis member broke, leaving the box stuck in gear. Jim Endruweit [Team Lotus's chief mechanic/racing manager] told Mike to go back out with the car in one gear and run around until it overheated and so we had an engine, and not a chassis, failure. The half-shaft broke in the race so there were a number of issues that weekend."

At Watkins Glen for the American Grand Prix, Spence became part of motor racing history. Shared drives had been part of the sport for aeons, largely because the races of yore were endurance marathons, often held in unbearable heat and beyond even the superhuman tolerance of some racing drivers, particularly the enthusiastic amateurs. Shared drives, of course, still exist to this day, in the long-distance sports car events like Le Mans, but in the World Championship, the races were getting shorter and thus the need for switching cars in a race was not quite a necessity as in previous years. Unless, of course, a World Championship title was at stake, as it was for Jim Clark.

Spence's race was relatively uneventful, albeit promising as he had moved up to a relatively strong fourth place. On lap 40, Clark's Lotus began to misfire when leading the race as

a result of a fuel injection problem. The system was adjusted and Clark dropped down the order. Mike's car was running well so he was called in to swap cars on lap fifty. Ultimately, the gamble did not work for Clark as he ended up finishing seventh when he ran out of fuel. Spence kept Clark's faulty car going for four more laps before the fuel injection system failed completely. The swap made this race the last ever Formula One race in which drivers shared the same car.

Lynne, Mike's widow, told me that contrary, to his easy-going nature and seemingly unabated support of the team, that Mike told her "that he accepted it as he saw the bigger picture but he was not happy." Realistically, looking at it with hindsight, it is little wonder Mike was vexed. If Clark had retired in his own car and the race played out as it did, then Mike could easily have finished a morale-boosting third and possibly even in second place as he was not too far behind the Ferrari of John Surtees at the time of his enforced pitstop. Surtees, towards the end of the race, spun trying to lap a backmarker, finishing some way down on race winner Graham Hill, so Mike could well have pipped him to finish as runner-up in the race.

That all being said, Mike very definitely was ready to play the team card at the next race, the Mexican Grand Prix of 1964, the last race of the year. Three drivers could win the

Mike at the German Grand Prix, 1964. *Etienne Bourguignon*

Mike in his Lotus. *Peter Darley*

World Championship: Jim Clark (Lotus), Graham Hill (BRM) and John Surtees (Ferrari). With Graham Hill five points ahead of Surtees and nine ahead of Clark, it was a tall order for the Lotus man to become World Champion. In order to win the title, Clark had to win the race, with Surtees finishing not higher than third and Hill not higher than fourth. Surtees could only win the title by finishing first, in each case, or second, unless Hill finished as high as third.

After a dramatic race which had already seen John Surtees' loyal Ferrari team-mate Lorenzo Bandini collide with Graham Hill somewhat unethically, damaging Hill's exhaust pipe and leaving him languishing well down the order, Jim Clark came through as the leader and on the way to the title. On the penultimate lap, his oil line failed and the engine seized. Mike, lying in fifth place at the time, seriously considered, at his own volition and in detriment to his own placing in the race, to nudge Clark's car around the circuit to try and keep him in first place. However, when everyone realised that Dan Gurney in the Brabham was too close behind and would take first place, Spence carried on and took a fine fourth. Graham Hill was about to become World Champion again but Bandini, then in second, dropped back to third, allowing John Surtees to take the title on the last lap by just one point from Hill. It remains one of the most dramatic conclusions to a World Championship season.

The season that had elevated Mike into the highest echelon of the sport finished in South Africa for the non-championship Rand Grand Prix, held at Kyalami a couple of weeks before Christmas. Again, I'll hand over to someone else to talk about the event and there is no better man than three-time World Champion and racing legend, Sir Jackie Stewart to reminisce: "One of the big events for me in the earlier part of my career is when I drove the South African Grand Prix for Lotus when Jimmy slipped his disc. He was at a ski resort called Cortina d'Ampezzo as they were launching a new Ford Cortina and then he slipped when throwing snowballs, as you do!

"He couldn't do the Rand Grand Prix and so Colin rang me and asked if I would like to race? I had already signed for BRM, of course, for the 1965 season. I said to Colin that I'd love to do it but I am under contract for next year. He asked me when the contract started and in actual fact, the contract did not start until January. So Colin rang Tony Rudd [Author note: Team principal at BRM and someone else who will feature more in this book in time]. Now Colin was a very convincing man when in full-flowing conversation 'It is a great opportunity for you guys as it will give Jackie Stewart experience in a Formula One race before the first Formula One race' and so on, so that Colin got what he

A happier Mike on the grid for the 1964 Austrian Grand Prix at Zeltweg.
Bill Cowe

wanted." [Author note: This would be Stewart's Formula One debut after dominating Formula Three that year.]

"Well, the car was amazing. Mike was very competitive in it. The Lotus felt like its centre of gravity was six inches underneath the tarmacadam as it had so much grip, and of course, in comparison, the BRM, when I tested it at lot at Snetterton, it felt like the centre of gravity was half an inch above the ground! The Lotus was just amazing, and of course, in those days, there was no aerodynamics *per se*, it was just geometry.

"So it got to the first heat as there were two heats overall. Typical Chapman. I put the car on pole and the driveshaft broke at the start. I was doing everything the right way, had the right revs, bang, broke. It was eye-opening and a wake-up call for me. I won the second heat but because of the start-line failure in the first race, I only finished seventeenth overall.

"I was very happy to be at BRM because my relationship with Graham Hill was different – and would have been different than had I been with Jimmy Clark. With Jim, in a funny kind of way, our friendship with each other stayed stronger because we weren't racing against each other in the same car."

Mike, who finished second in the first heat at Kyalami, but had to retire with a broken rosejoint in the second heat, had certainly shown that in his relatively rapid rise up the racing ladder, that he had the ability and flexibility to adapt and had at least earned a chance to keep his seat for 1965. But he was well aware that he needed to really show his mettle in his first full season with the team. He well and truly did that with aplomb at the start of 1965.

Brands Awareness

"I have very fond memories of Mike. Mike was an excellent
team man, versatile and enthusiastic and very loyal.
He got on well with everybody and never whinged once"
Bob Dance, Lotus mechanic

Lorenzo Bandini, Jim Clark, Colin Chapman, Mike Spence and Lynne Condon (later to be Lynne Spence), 1965 South African Grand Prix.

Mike Spence/Lynne Spence

The two Lotus cars in the pits at the 1965 South African Grand Prix. Colin Chapman (red hat) sits on the pit wall. *Mike Spence/Lynne Spence*

Mike on the grid for the South African Grand Prix. *Lynne Spence*

The 1965 season started promisingly for Mike and Team Lotus. At the South African Grand Prix, held at the East London circuit on New Year's Day, Mike was close behind Jim Clark as the two Lotus team-mates ran first and second for the majority of the race, with Mike qualifying on the second row. Mike had a spin at the hairpin twice (he had a torrid time with that hairpin as he spun three times in successive laps during practice) and eventually finished fourth. Despite that, Mike was being noticed by a number of people. Tony Rudd of BRM recalled in his book *It was Fun!*: "We noticed that Spence, the Lotus number two driver, was developing into a driver nearly as quick as Clark when his car held together".

But the next race, two months later, was even more successful. The grandly-titled Race of Champions was a new event, held over two heats of 40 laps each of the Brands Hatch circuit in Kent. The first heat was straightforward enough. Jim Clark won ahead of Dan Gurney's Brabham with Mike in third place. For the second heat, Dan Gurney made the best start but all Jim Clark had to do to win on

aggregate was simply to follow the American. But Jim Clark was not normally a driver to settle for second if he could win and the two leaders got into a scrap for the lead.

On lap 12, under pressure from Gurney, Clark made an uncharacteristic mistake and went wide on the grass. The car hit some ruts that pitched it into the grass banking. Clark, unhurt but winded, was out. Then Gurney retired due to ignition failure. Mike came through and won the heat and aggregate victory ahead of, respectively, Jo Bonnier's Brabham and Jackie Stewart's BRM. Although luck had played its part, the win was very much deserved and impressed many. Alan Brinton, a journalist who spent thirty years in the sport and was a former editor of *Motor Racing News*, wrote in *The Observer* newspaper in May 1965 comparing Spence to the rising star of the sport, Jackie Stewart. 'Spence has shown his consistency and Stewart has dazzled everyone. I shall be surprised if at least one of these two drivers is not high in the championship table when the season ends in Mexico City. Although each is running as number two in their team, they have revealed that each is perfectly capable of taking over if the number ones hit trouble.'

Colin Chapman explains something to Jim Clark and Mike, who nibbles away on a cheeseburger at the same time! *Lynne Spence*

Mike at the 1965 South African Grand Prix. *Roger Swan/David Pearson* (www.motoprint.co.za)

Before the Race of Champions event - from left to right: Jochen Rindt, John Taylor, Jo Bonnier (background), Mike Spence and Ian Raby. The change between the more modern professional driver and the veterans of the 1950's is obvious in this picture when you compare Rindt and Raby and their choice of outfit. *Peter Darley*

A happy man! *Peter Darley*

Upon his return to Maidenhead, where Spence now lived, he told the local paper, the *Maidenhead Advertiser* that "I knew I was in with a chance. I finished with the third fastest time in practice and was at the front of the grid at the start. Now I feel very happy."

The next Championship race would normally have been the Monaco Grand Prix, however Team Lotus did not participate in the race. This was not because Jim Clark was racing (and winning) at the Indianapolis 500, as Lotus had proved they could split themselves up into different divisions with no overall detriment. It was actually because they boycotted the race due to that fact that, to quote team manager Andrew Ferguson, "Our team was assured of only one place on the starting grid, although we signed an agreement with organisers of the World Championship events stipulating that factory-entered autos would always get two places."

In retrospect, you have to wonder if this would have been Mike's best chance of winning a World Championship event. There was no Jim Clark and no Dan Gurney, and Mike

Mike Spence in the Lotus 33 at the 1965 South African Grand Prix.
Roger Swan/David Pearson (www.motoprint.co.za)

was in the designated number one car with Pedro Rodriguez due to back him up in the second car.

By the time of the next championship grand prix, at Belgium's Spa Francorchamps circuit in mid-June, Mike had been busy in both non-championship events and Formula Two. His best results were at the Eifelrennen Formula Two race at the Nürburgring and at the non-championship BRDC International Trophy at Silverstone, where he finished third at both events. He was also very quick at the non-championship Glover Trophy at Goodwood, qualifying second just 0.2sec behind Jim Clark. However, any hopes of challenging failed on the warm-up lap when his metering unit failed.

However, in championship events, the results weren't coming together after the early success. He finished out of the points in Belgium and then at the next race at France. In mitigation, Mike was in a solid fifth place before injection pump failure led to a spin which pitched him down to eighth. He soon moved up into seventh but was compromised by a misfiring engine for the rest of the race.

When it came to the British Grand Prix, where he finished a fine fourth, Mike's reputation was still extremely positive. In the preview of the British Grand Prix of 1965, Stirling Moss reviewed the drivers ahead of the race for *Car* magazine. The legendary driver's review of Mike was as follows: "Every driver likes a good team-mate to back him up and Clark's got a good one in Spence. In a way, Clark is doubly lucky, after Arundell's tragic crash and illness, to find such a good man so soon."

The next real event of note was at Pergusa, for the Mediterranean Grand Prix. Mike was in a strong second place behind Jo Siffert in his Brabham-BRM fighting nose-to-tail at the high-speed circuit. Then Jim Clark caught the pair and Mike was told firstly to hold in second place and then

Mike in the Ron Harris Team Lotus Formula Two car at the Eifelrennen race at the Nürburgring. **Nils Ruwisch archive**

to let Jim through. Spence eased off and Clark moved into second. Clark's car then inadvertently flicked up a stone that smashed into the bridge of Mike's nose. Temporarily blinded, with his eyes streaming with tears of pain, Mike veered off the circuit at 140mph, ran wide and clipped the straw bales. This pitched his car into a spin across the other side of the track where his car then toppled over the grass bank (there were no run-off areas, of course, in the 1960s) and went upside down in the lake in the dense reeds.

The lake had welcomed Mike Hailwood a year before, with the legendary motorcyclist-turned-race car driver getting a thorough soaking but he was, at least, the right way up. However, this time, there was concern as the top of Mike's crash helmet was in the water and if that was not fun enough, poisonous snakes resided in the lake.

Marshals gathered around the car but 'jabbered away without making any attempt to right the car' to quote Doug

Nye in *Motor Sport*. Team Lotus mechanics Bill Cowe and Leo Wybrott realised what had happened. Wybrott later recalled to *Motor Sport* magazine: "We had a vague idea of where Mike must be so we set off, running back around the circuit on the infield. We ran a long way but all that time he was trapped upside down under the car in the bulrushes, slowly sinking down into the water. When we found him, he was still in the car and the marshals were standing about. We just jumped in and must have woken the marshals into finally helping. We retrieved the car but it was not damaged, just wet! Mike was peeved to say the least." As Bill Cowe recalled to me, even this marshalling fiasco did not make mild-mannered Mike apoplectic with rage. "I can't imagine Mike ever being angry. I don't recall this incident too well but I would have remembered it, without doubt, if Mike was angry!" Siffert eventually won from Clark by just 0.3sec.

Mike with Peter Revson and Paul Hawkins at the Eifelrennen Formula Two race at the Nürburgring. **Günther Kever/archive Nils Ruwisch**

The Ron Harris Team Lotus outfit. In the background is a young Peter Revson. The man furthest back in the trailer is Malcolm Angood. **Lynne Spence**

Spence and Revson chat while waiting to race in the Formula Two race at
Crystal Palace. *Lynne Spence*

Mike in the Lotus 33. *Bill Cowe*

Mike at the Belgian Grand Prix, 1965. *Etienne Bourguignon*

Jim Clark and Mike relax in the paddock. *Clive Talbot/Andy Talbot Media*

Mike in the Lotus awaiting the race start. *Peter Darley*

Jim and Mike wait in the pits at the Belgian Grand Prix, 1965. *John Spence*

Lynne Spence finds that motor racing is not always enjoyable and glamorous. "I can't remember where it was but it was bloody cold and I was fed up!"
Lynne Spence

Mike in the Lotus 33 at the 1965 Belgian Grand Prix. *Etienne Bourguignon*

Mike in the Lotus at the Belgian Grand Prix, 1965. *Etienne Bourguignon*

Mike explaining an issue to mechanic Leo Wybrott. *Etienne Bourguignon*

Mike and Jim Clark in conversation with Geoff Murdoch, competitions manager of Esso. *Peter Darley*

Mike and Jim Clark enjoy choc ices before the 1965 Belgian Grand Prix. *Etienne Bourguignon*

Mike at the British Grand Prix, 1965. *John Spence*

Mike's luck with the reliability of his car started to go downhill. Transmission failure at the German Grand Prix was followed by an alternator problem late on in the Italian Grand Prix. The next championship race at Watkins Glen for the American Grand Prix saw only nine laps completed before engine failure intervened. There was obvious deep frustration for all, not least, if Colin Chapman is to be believed, that Mike had the quicker car of the two Lotus drivers. Chapman's thoughts were in Karl Ludvigsen's book about Colin Chapman titled *Inside the Innovator*: "Starting in 1964, Climax produced a 32-valve version, and was released to Lotus in 1965. When we first used the four-valve engine, Jim Clark felt it was quicker for one reason only – it carburetted better – but they never did get much power out of it. We had a two-valve engine which Mike Spence used most of the season which has always been within one or two horsepower of it. Every time Climax got an increase on the four-valve, they could go back and get it onto the two-valve for the same reason. Towards the end of the season Jimmy was not sure if it carburetted better and he could almost always jump into

Mike's car and go quicker. I would say Mike had the quicker car most of 1965.'

The final race of the season was the Mexican Grand Prix in a race won by Richie Ginther in the Honda. Mike's race was a very good one and, at one point, having passed Jackie Stewart, was starting to close in on a dominant, but car-conserving Ginther, eventually finishing in an excellent third place.

Spence had been consistently successful all season and the team were impressed by his dedication to the team and the meticulous and conscientious way he looked after the cars. However, his performances had not quite compared to Peter Arundell's brilliant but all-too-brief early success of 1964. Although Mike had done little wrong, Chapman honoured his promise made to Arundell when the Englishman was recovering in hospital that when he was fit enough, he would get his seat back. In retrospect it was the wrong decision, but a wholly honourable one.

If Mike was irked by being dropped by Lotus for Arundell, he certainly did not show it. A philosophical statement was

Mike in the car at the British Grand Prix, 1965. *Peter Darley*

Mike Spence and Jim Clark. *Peter Darley*

made by him in early 1966 to the *Reading Evening Post*, one that was pretty consistent with other statements over the years: "Eventually, every driver's ambition is to be World Champion. But I always enjoy racing just for the fun of it." In fact, he was relishing racing alongside Jim Clark in their forthcoming Formula Two drives in the Ron Harris Team Lotus team. "It's good to stay with Jim. Jim is a terrific team-mate and he is always willing to help you along. I learned a lot from following him into corners."

By and large, there was only positive feedback for Mike from the Lotus mechanics and other observers of the sport as the below feedback from mostly Team Lotus employees shows.

Jim Endruweit, chief mechanic, recalled to Paul Fearnley for *Motor Sport* magazine: "Mike was neat and tidy, easy on the car. But it's possible he was overawed. In some ways, it did not matter who was our number two. We had two cars but it's no surprise Jimmy was the focus. His car had to be

Spence and Clark share a joke. *Edgar Vernon Starr/Guy Loveridge and Tim Beavis*

110 percent whilst the other could get by on at 100 percent. If the number two kicked off, he might not have got as much 'service with a smile'."

Sir Jackie Stewart: "Mike was a shy, well mannered, modest but very nice man. A really nice man. He suffered from being at Lotus at the same time as Jim, as did a lot of other people, of course, like Peter Arundell and so on. He was a good driver but he was not a *great* driver, but of course, there's not many of them around. And of course, the trouble is, when you are in the same team as Jim Clark, who was a great driver, you did not have much of a chance.

"Chapman could choose good people and indeed he did so, but while Jim was there... that's one of the reasons I never went to Lotus because first of all, the cars were considerably more fragile than everybody else's. But secondly, as long as Jim Clark was there, there was one man who was going to be cared for in first class fashion. I chose BRM instead of Lotus. I never said yes to Colin, he asked me more than once, but although he was a brilliant engineer of creative fast cars, his cars were more fragile. Even the Elite and the Elans, let alone a Formula One or Formula Two car were more fragile than other ones. So Mike had to play second fiddle to Jim Clark wherever he went when he was at Lotus. Jimmy was the golden boy, which he deserved to be, but Colin had him on a pedestal.

"I remember when Jochen Rindt went there and he was horrified by some of the stuff that was on the Lotus car. There were bits and pieces from Triumph Heralds on there. There were little bits and pieces that Colin chose to have that Tony Rudd would not have had or Jack Brabham would not have had or Ken Tyrrell would not have had. So it was a difficult time for Mike. I don't think Trevor Taylor, Arundell or Spence ever reached their true potential as they were driving a car that had a number one driver who was the best of his kind. In Colin's head everyone else was second-rate."

Mike in the German Grand Prix at the Nürburgring, 1965. *Etienne Bourguignon*

Mike at the Nürburgring, German Grand Prix, 1965. *John Spence*

Dick Scammell, Jim Clark's mechanic and later Team Lotus racing manager: "Mike did a very good job. It was very open with him and Jimmy. No secrets were kept. He was a very nice gentleman and a pleasant person to be around. He worked *so* hard for the success of the team. He put the success of the team ahead of himself and he enjoyed the combined successes together.

"He had a little bit more technical feedback than some other drivers. But the way Team Lotus worked in those days, drivers gave the feedback from driving around and we, and by we I mean mostly Colin, made the decision. Jimmy was excellent at feedback too and because he was so good at what he did, he could tell Colin exactly how he wanted it. However, neither Jim nor Mike, no matter how good they were at what they did, engineered or designed the cars."

Doug Nye, esteemed motor racing author and historian: "Spence was one of the most underrated drivers. Among engineers and mechanics at BRM and Lotus he was held in great affection and respect. He was a super development driver." David Porter responded to the underrated comments in a Shell motorsport profile booklet in 1967. 'This underrated tag seems to be largely an attitude of the press. At least the people who matter haven't underrated him.'

Bob Dance: "I have very fond memories of Mike. He was a cheerful pleasant man, very enthusiastic and a very good driver. Versatile too, which was very important in those days because you had to be capable of driving anything while you were with Lotus. He got on well with everyone and was an all-round good bloke. As a development driver, he was quite useful actually. He was very interested in the development of the cars and understanding the car. He gave quite good feedback. He learnt from some of the best – I mean, he worked with Colin Chapman, Jim Clark and Jack Sears, who were all brilliant in their field. That helped him develop as well with us.

"Mike was an excellent team man. Very loyal, very good to the team. He was a good team-mate and a good team person. He got on well with everybody – Jim Clark, Colin Chapman,

Paul Hawkins (left) and Mike Spence. *Lynne Spence*

Mike at Silverstone, 1965. *Peter Darley*

Colin Chapman, Jim Clark and Mike Spence at the US Grand Prix, 1965 at Watkins Glen. *Bruce Wennerstrom/John Spence*

A thoughtful Mike with a young Jochen Rindt behind him. *Peter Darley*

Mike at the 1965 BRDC International Trophy at Silverstone. *Peter Darley*

The Lotus team relax at the Hotel Maria Isabel during the time away at the Mexican Grand Prix 1965. As well as Jim, Mike and Colin Chapman, there's a young David Hobbs (fifth left) and Hazel Chapman, Colin's wife (third right). *Bill Cowe*

Mike leads Dan Gurney at the 1965 Mexican Grand Prix. **Ted Walker**

Dick Scammell, David Lazenby (another former Clark race mechanic who later became components manager at Lotus). Never whinged once, or not that I ever saw."

Bob Sparshott: "I remember Mike with great affection, he was a good character. Quintessential Englishman, quite reserved but a very good driver indeed."

Mike appeared to never have any real issue being a number two driver, at least not at Lotus. Bill Gavin, in his *Autosport* article about Mike in 1965, revealed the following after discussion with Mike: "His lot of number two driver he doesn't resent. He gets on very well with Jimmy Clark and speaks highly of Colin Chapman's fairness to him."

Mike's fondness and support for Jim Clark remained the whole way through his career. In an interview in *Motor Racing* magazine in late 1967, he was asked if there were any drivers he admired. "Yes, Jimmy Clark. I think he's far and away above any of the others, both in his driving and in his approach as a professional. I do also admire those who try really hard but Jim has natural genius."

So Mike was out at Lotus. But he would not have too much trouble finding another seat. As Doug Nye revealed in volume 3 of the *Saga of British Racing Motors*, many other teams had already eyed up Mike. On 1 November 1965, BRM grandee Raymond Mays wrote to Tim Parnell, looking forward to the 1966 season in which Parnell Racing would run with BRM support: "As you will know, one of the ideas of our tie-up with you has always been with a view of choosing an up and coming driver, so if good enough, he could be made use of for the BRM team. The point has to be taken into consideration next year that driving the 3.0 litres will be a very different matter from driving the existing one-and-a-half-litre cars and I rather feel that an experienced Formula One driver may be the answer for this first year of the new formula. In this case, it might well be advised seriously to consider Mike Spence. He is certainly a pretty good driver and he has vast experience of Lotus machines."

Parnell took the hint. It was time for Mike to join another iconic British racing team.

Mike in the Lotus 33 at the 1965 British Grand Prix. *Peter Darley*

Mike in conversation. *Peter Darley*

Mike in the Lotus. *Brooks Schwartz/Bill Cowe*

Mike in the Nurburgring pits, German Grand Prix, 1965.

Raimund Kommer

Mike in the car at the US Grand Prix, 1965. *Lynne Spence*

Win and Lynne

"Mike was not a ladies man, he was not a Graham Hill type with a twinkle in his eye, bless him, but he was a really nice guy with very lovely blue eyes"
Lynne Spence

Mike and Lynne Spence on their wedding day, 15 January 1966. *Lynne Spence*

Mike on his way to winning the 1966 South African Grand Prix. *John Spence*

Mike travelled to South Africa in December for an extended stay. This was both for personal and professional reasons. He was very keen to enter the Rand Grand Prix held on 4 December, but Team Lotus decided against entering this time out. The organisers tried in vain to find a drive, but could only rustle up an ancient Lotus 21 from former grand prix driver Neville Lederle. Knowing he would struggle and would be bringing unnecessary risk, Mike decided to sit out and watch the race as a spectator.

He stayed on and enjoyed Christmas in South Africa and was still in the country for the first Grand Prix of the year at East London, which as usual, was held on New Year's Day. This year, though, the race would be a non-championship event. What had happened at the end of 1965 is that sports cars were generally lapping faster than the so-called pinnacle of the sport Formula One cars, so the engine capacity changed from 1.5 litres to 3.0 litres accordingly.

Initially, the South African Grand Prix on 1 January 1966 was due to start the new 3.0-litre era. However, so many teams were struggling to have their cars ready in time that the race was downgraded to non-championship status. As it was, only one 3.0-litre car made it; Jack Brabham's BT19 with a Repco V8 engine. The other entries were a variation

Mike in the Lotus 33 leading the South African Grand Prix, 1966. *Lynne Spence*

of 2.8 litres (Prophet), 2.7 litres (Hulme, Hawkins, Anderson, Love, Tingle, Hume, de Klerk, Charlton and Puzey), 2.0 litres (Spence, Ginther, Ireland, Serrurier, Pretorius and Jefferies) and 1.5 litres (Bonnier and Arundell (back for the first time after his Reims crash). Jack Holme and Brian Reubenheimer had 1600cc Formula twin-cam engines in their cars – small wonder the race became a non-championship one with such a variation of entries.

This was Mike's last race for Team Lotus and he was in the Lotus 33 R11 car with a Coventry Climax V8 engine

A slightly overwhelmed Mike after winning the 1966 South African Grand Prix. *John Spence*

Mike and Lynne enjoy the celebrations of winning the 1966 South African Grand Prix. *Lynne Spence*

Tony Maggs, Lynne's one-time brother-in-law who introduced Mike and Lynne to each other. *Lynne Spence*

Lynne and Mike on their wedding day, 15 January 1966. *Lynne Spence*

Lynne and Mike are joined by Rev Bellis for photographs for their wedding day.
Lynne Spence

The wedding party from left to right: David Spence, Winifred Spence, Tony Maggs, Jim Meikle, Mike Spence, Lynne Spence, Gaile Condon (Lynne's sister), Kandy Condon (Lynne's cousin) and Mr and Mrs Condon (Lynne's parents).
Lynne Spence

intended solely to tide Lotus over until the first championship race, which now would not be until late May at Monaco. Peter Arundell would be Mike's team mate, but according to Doug Nye's *Theme Lotus* book he looked 'Pale faced still and had a limp'. Clearly, Pete was not back to his old self just yet but, after this race, he had another four months of recovery ahead until the Monaco Grand Prix.

In practice, with the obvious advantage of being the only person with a 3.0-litre engine, Jack Brabham took pole position. Mike was second with Denny Hulme, albeit with more power, a close third. John Love was fourth with Innes Ireland and Richie Ginther fifth and sixth respectively. A clearly uncomfortable Arundell was 13th.

Mike made an excellent start to pull ahead and lead from Brabham and Hulme, helped somewhat by drizzle before the race better suiting his tyre compound. One lap later, though, Brabham retook the lead. Soon the rain stopped and, with the warm temperatures helping, the track dried quickly. Not enough for Richie Ginther who slid off, caught out by a wetter part of the track in his BRP.

Brabham held a relatively secure 5.0sec lead over Mike, with Spence holding around the same margin over Hulme. Just after half way through the race, Hulme's transmission failed after the gearbox, which was now only in second gear, let go completely. This meant that Mike had a big gap to the new third-place runner Piet de Klerk and it helped Peter Arundell climb up the order.

With eleven laps to go, Brabham retired when his fuel injection pump failed and Mike coasted home to win by two laps. He had been fortunate, there's no question about it, but he had more or less kept pace with Brabham the whole way through where no-one else had. Peter Arundell came a morale-boosting third, described by Nye as 'Tired, stiff but smiling'.

Mike was greeted by a number of people at the finish but made a beeline for one in particular, his South African fiancée Lynne. Mike had revealed to the *Reading Evening Post* in October 1965 news of his forthcoming nuptials: "I will go over to South Africa both to race and to see my fiancée Lynne, who I will marry after Christmas. But I hope to be back here [Maidenhead] a little more often after I get married. I shall being bringing Lynne back with me to live here."

Lynne Condon was just 19 but had been around the racing circuits in her homeland for some years. Her elder sister Gaile was married to Tony Maggs and it was Maggs who had semi-introduced Lynne to Mike, although as Lynne explains she was familiar with Mike anyway.

"I had always been interested in motor racing through my father and I was a junior go-kart champion at the age of 12, so there was always an interest in cars. As a result, I was always around the pits, especially as my sister Gaile was married to Tony Maggs. In those days, you wandered freely in the pits. Either my sister or maybe Anthony [Maggs] introduced us to each other at Kyalami on 12 December 1964.

"In early 1965, Gail and Tony rented a house at Hartebeestpoort Dam where some of the racing drivers used to stay during their leisure time. I used to go there at the weekend with my parents to water-ski. Michael was staying there at the time so I got to know him a lot better. In February 1965, Mike asked if I would like to go with him to Australia

to visit his parents. 'No strings attached,' he said, so I thought 'yes that sounds rather nice,' and off we went.

"I met his lovely parents and had a wonderful few weeks there. We went back to Maidenhead in March and that was when he won the Race of Champions. We got engaged mid-year and I returned to South Africa to finalise plans for our wedding. Mike joined me there after the Mexico Grand Prix in October 1965. His win at East London was a nice early wedding present for us. We returned to Australia for another short stay after our wedding, and then on to our honeymoon in Hawaii before starting a hectic few years, where I was now the wife of a racing driver.

"I was attracted by Mike's very lovely blue eyes. He was not a ladies man, he was not a Graham Hill type with a twinkle in his eye, bless him, but he was a really nice guy. In those days you got married. It was the thing to do. For our wedding day in Pretoria, Mike's parents came over from Australia. Jim Meikle was there as Mike's best man and I think Tony [Maggs] was the only driver. It went by in a bit of a blur but

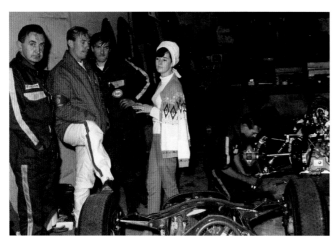

Mike and Lynne in the pits of the Reg Parnell Lotus-BRM team at the German Grand Prix, Nürburgring, 1966. *Nils Ruwisch archive*

Lynne and Mike Spence. *Peter Darley*

Not so much watching the wheels, but washing them. A driver's wife would sometimes do far more than just watch. Not much chance of seeing this in modern Formula One! *Nils Ruwisch archive*

as I recall it was a beautiful day with gorgeous weather. Very soon after that we came over to Maidenhead.

"After the wedding day, we went to Australia to where Mike's parents lived. They were fantastic people. I think I admired them more than I admired anyone else ever in my entire life. They, until their dying day, kept in touch with me and treated me as their daughter. Not as their daughter-in-law, but as if I was their actual daughter. They sent Christmas cards, they never once forgot a birthday. They were both truly wonderful people.

"I went to every race with Mike. I think the only real time we had at Maidenhead was during the winter testing time because it was off to one race, then back, then preparing for the next one, then off we went. We did not really have any time there at all. If I did, I washed his overalls, cleaned the goggles – he was always obsessive about his goggles as he wanted them to fit just right and be really clean – and there was no real time to properly relax. We had a darling little cottage called Bella Vista Cottage in Sheephouse Road, Maidenhead, which was about five minutes from the town centre but in a very pleasant area. It was a woodland cottage which was situated one street back from the River Thames. It would have had a beautiful garden if we had the time to look after it. Then later on we lived in a place in nearby Bray called Braybank. David Porter stayed on at Bella Vista Cottage in a grace-and-favour arrangement."

Mike also confirmed that time to enjoy home comforts in Maidenhead was limited in the aforementioned interview in October 1965 to the *Reading Evening Post*: "I have been popping in and out again. I was in Mexico, then New York with Jimmy Clark for a couple of presentations, then London, then over to South Africa. I do not get a chance to spend very much time in Maidenhead. I always seem to be somewhere else, usually racing abroad. At the moment I am more or less living from week to week and never quite know what's going to happen next."

Mike and Lynne were married on 15 January 1966 in Pretoria, at the Wesley Methodist Church, with the service presided by the Reverend R Bellis. Gaile and Kandy Condon [Kandy was Lynne's cousin – her paternal uncle's daughter] were the bridesmaids and then, as Lynne says above, they went to Australia before settling down, in a manner of words, in Maidenhead.

May 1966 saw a very unwelcome disturbance to the couple's idyllic home. On 7 May 1966, as Mike and Lynne slept at their cottage, thieves broke into the garage, stole and then crashed his gold Ferrari 2.0-litre 250 GT car, which he had owned for only a week before the incident. The car was a write-off, losing Mike some £3000 (£47,000 in today's money). They stole wheels and other equipment,

An apparently dejected Mike is consoled by Lynne. **Lynne Spence**

before dumping it in the woods at Burnham Beeches near Slough, nine miles away. Upon bringing the car back to a workshop, Mike said, "The thing was absolutely wrecked. They have done at least £500 worth of damage. The carburettors and the air hose have been taken off as well as various other bits and pieces which they tore right out of their roots. They also removed the wheels and left the car on the ground on its axle stubs and body work. I doubt if those responsible will be able to sell the things they have taken because of the very limited number of such cars in this country and they cannot be fitted to any other type of car. The only thing I can think is that these people did not know what they were doing."

Generally, though, the couple adapted to married life as best they could, with Lynne choosing to attend every race Mike competed at. This was for a number of reasons, but one of the main contributing factors to this decision was the realisation that if Lynne did not travel with Mike, that they would barely see one another. As Lynne was already interested in motor racing, the decision was an easy one.

Mike's very next race after his win and wedding in South Africa, competing in a 2.0-litre sports car race, saw another victory. Racing in his first event for the Parnell-BRM outfit at the BARC International Lavant Cup at Goodwood, Mike won after 21 laps at an average speed of 97.78mph, with Tony Dean in his Brabham BT8-Climax powered engine 2.5sec behind.

One month later, he took his third and final win of the season, the Anerley Trophy at Crystal Palace which was the Parnell-BRM's second race, and second win. Starting in pole position, he took a comfortable win with a lead of 21 seconds after twenty laps from future Grand Prix driver Peter Gethin, racing a Crossle-BMW. That, unfortunately, was pretty much the last race of the year that Mike enjoyed substantial success. The rest of the next year-and-a-half's association with BRM would test Mike's patience and good spirits to the maximum.

Not Sweet H16

"Mike Spence was, without any doubt in my mind, the most technically brilliant of all drivers"
Tim Parnell, former BRM team manager

Mike Spence in the BRM H16 at the 1967 South African Grand Prix. *Ken Stewart/David Pearson (www.motoprint.co.za)*

With the 1966 season all over the place in terms of engine capacity and new technical regulations, an assortment of machinery was cobbled together. Mike now mainly drove a Lotus 33 for Tim Parnell with a 2.0-litre Tasman BRM engine. From being at one of the top teams, Mike was now pretty much an also-ran.

The Lotus 33 was the effective successor to the Lotus 25. A logical development to the monocoque car, it had stronger and stiffer, but also a lighter chassis and it used the latest wide wheels and tyres. "Oh yes, it was going to be a lot quicker too" said designer Len Terry to author Doug Nye in his book *Theme Lotus*. Terry developed the car around Dunlop tyres, removing any excess weight – not that there was much fat to be trimmed.

Very early on, it became clear things weren't going to go well. No 3.0-litre engines were available for him until mid-season as the BRM factory very swiftly realised that new engines were unlikely to be ready for their own works team, and as a result, driving for Parnell, he would be handicapped with a 2.0-litre engine. The smallest iota of frustration, rare from Mike, spilled out in an interview with the *Reading Evening Post* in 1966. "You can't compete seriously like that. It's very disappointing, but at least the engine has proved reliable and it is mounted in a known chassis. I would like to improve my results but it all depends on when the engines are ready. We were expecting some trouble in getting a fully competitive car, particularly at the start of the season. Even some of the works teams are in the same position."

Tim Parnell pretty much grew up in the sport. Tim was the son of Reg Parnell, a farmer and proprietor of a haulage business in Derbyshire, who had raced in the 1930s, including at Brooklands at Donington Park. Banned for two years for a misjudged overtaking move on Kay Petre, which left the famed female driver with serious injuries, Reg Parnell lent

29 May 1967 – Mike Spence and Tim Parnell at the London Trophy Formula Two race, Brands Hatch. **Chris Beach**

cars to other drivers and learnt how to manage the stock. During World War Two, Parnell stored a number of racing cars for safety at his Derbyshire farm, which Tim played around with as a boy, with much zeal and gusto. Reg Parnell, then post-war, became one of Britain's leading racing drivers and finished third in the very first World Championship race at Silverstone in 1950.

Reg was not keen on Tim racing, but Parnell junior would not be deterred. He began his own career in 1957 and Reg soon understood that the racing bug had well and truly bitten, and subsequently supported his son. Parnell raced in Formula Junior, Formula Two, sports cars and then in Formula One, attempted qualification between 1959 and 1963. Parnell was probably not as talented as his father, but tragedy struck before a full analysis could be made. Reg Parnell, by now running his own successful racing team, died suddenly of peritonitis at the age of just 52 in the first week of 1964, when, while being treated for a heavy cold in hospital, an embolism formed in his leg.

Mike in the Parnell-BRM at the Anerley Trophy, Crystal Palace, 30 May 1966.
John Adams (Racebears)

Mike in the Parnell-Lotus BRM, 1966 at the BRDC International Trophy.
Timothy Reid/John Spence

Mike leads Jo Siffert at the 1966 Monaco Grand Prix. *Etienne Bourguignon*

It was left for Tim not just to mourn his father but to take over the team in the most appalling of circumstances. Through his association with BRM, plumping for their engines instead of the Coventry-Climax alternatives, Parnell built up a good relationship with them as a privateer owner and then, in 1969, he replaced Lotus-bound Tony Rudd as BRM's team manager, a role he remained in for six largely torrid seasons. A big, bluff fellow, Tim remained linked to the sport for a long time, serving as the vice president of the British Racing Drivers' Club for seven years until 2010.

Sadly, Parnell's health took a downturn shortly after that. I met Tim just the once at the Race Retro event in February 2013. He had lost a lot of weight and was noticeably frailer, but he was dignified, modest and very down-to-earth and happy to chat to anyone who recognised him. Tim died on 5 April 2017.

Richard Attwood: "Basically, driving one of Tim's cars was really a complete waste of time because they were two or, in my case, three years old and were not competitive anywhere. Tim was an affable sort of guy and very easy to get along with, and I suppose he was living the dream being involved with an F1 team."

Alan Challis, long time BRM mechanic recalled to Doug Nye for his Volume 3 of the *Saga of British Racing Motors*: "Tim was a leading private owner who, like all customers, was a pain. They were always on the cadge, getting something for nothing. But Tim was always very friendly and nice. You just knew he was always trying to charm something out of us. It could irritate us to be constantly touched for bits and assistance. But Tim had grown up in racing and it was his way

of life. We respected him for that. In effect, he'd been involved longer in the sport than all the rest us had been."

Mike's association with Parnell allowed a bit more flexibility to drive alternative machinery for numerous individuals. His season started badly in one of the more well known outfits, the Matra Formula Two cars run by soon-to-be legendary Formula One team boss Ken Tyrrell. Racing at Barcelona at the Montjuic Park circuit, he had to take evasive action when a spectator suddenly fell off a straw bale right in front of him. Given a choice of killing the spectator or crashing, Mike swerved and drove into a wall. He suffered a badly bruised foot, one of his very few injuries sustained in his entire career. It ruled him out of the next non-championship Formula One event at Syracuse one week later.

Mike returned three weeks after his crash but was an early retiree at the International Trophy at Silverstone when the BRM engine failed after just five laps. Disappointment followed at Monaco. Lying sixth at around the one-third distance mark, the rear suspension collapsed. "Fortunately, it happened at the slowest point of the circuit – the 25mph Station hairpin bend just before coming onto the sea front straight – but it could've been pretty awkward," he said on his return home to the *Maidenhead Advertiser*.

A string of retirements followed in the Parnell-Lotus, with occasional drives elsewhere, including with Richard Bond at the Nürburgring 1000km and a return to Ron Harris in Formula Two, finishing fourth at Reims. But Mike's determination continued. He took a quite brilliant fifth place at Zandvoort at the Dutch Grand Prix in July, in a car painted in white with a green stripe, which was doubling up for Pete

Mike's overalls say 'Scott' for filming the film *Grand Prix*. Brian Bedford's character was called Scott Stoddard. ***Bernard Cahier/Lynne Spence***

Mike puts on his goggles, German Grand Prix 1966. ***Nils Ruwisch archive***

Mike in the pits at the Nürburgring, 1966 German Grand Prix.

Nils Ruwisch archive

Actor Brian Bedford relaxes during filming of the film *Grand Prix*. Spence would often be Bedford's driving double. ***Mike Spence/Lynne Spence***

Mike Spence and David Hobbs at the Nine Hours of Kyalami race, 1966. They were entered by Bernard White. ***Ken Stewart/David Pearson***

(www.motoprint.co.za)

The German Grand Prix, 1966. Jo Bonnier leads Denny Hulme (4), Mike (15) and Ludovico Scarfiotti. Also in the picture is Alan Rees (29) in the Brabham and Jean-Pierre Beltoise (34) in the Matra. *Sigurd Reilbach*

Aron's Yamura car for MGM's *Grand Prix* film. Spence's normal distinctive helmet was ditched as he drove around in a white helmet with red and blue vertical stripes, which was a reverse of Chris Amon's helmet design.

At the British Grand Prix, Parnell was again approached to have his Lotus-BRM painted red this time to look like a Ferrari and Mike was persuaded to wear another different crash helmet with red dashes so that he looked like Ferrari driver Mike Parkes. However, by the time another paint job was required at the Italian Grand Prix, Parnell's first wife, Ginny, recalled to Alan Henry for *Motor Sport* magazine that "The car was sprayed so many times that when they finally wanted it repainted white to look like Yamura again, there was so much red paint already on it that it turned out pink!"

The Italian Grand Prix saw another fifth place which was realistically the optimum position he could challenge for. A largely fruitless year was summed up by the Mexican Grand Prix, the last race of the season when Mike did not even start the race. A hub bolt dropped from the front suspension, which then in turn led to the wheel and brake caliper falling off. But despite this, Mike was never too down and angry, according to Parnell who spoke a few decades later to Paul Fearnley at *Motor Sport* magazine. "There was no side to Mike, he just got on with it. He was very kind to his machinery and he had great technical sense," Around the same time, Parnell spoke

in length about Mike to Karl Ludvigsen for his book, *Colin Chapman: Inside the Innovator*. "Spence was, without any doubt in my mind, the most technically brilliant of all drivers. If we were testing a car or setting one up and qualifying for a race, after a couple of laps on the track Mike would come in to say that this or that was wrong or some changes were needed with settings.

The mechanics worked on the car to his stipulations and off he went again. You could bet your bottom dollar that the following laps were instantly quicker. He was a great technical man and a terrific asset to the team. I don't really think that Colin Chapman wanted to lose him; he appreciated what a good test driver he was. It was that knowledge of his testing abilities that gave way to Colin Chapman choosing him to drive in the 1968 Indianapolis 500."

The last race of Mike's 1966 season came at Kyalami for the 9-Hour race in a Ford GT40 sharing the drive with David Hobbs. Hobbs remembered this race very well, and he also remembered the team owner, Bernard White. Again, I'll hand over to someone else and, in this case, it is the seasoned television commentator to take us through the race and his memories of Bernard White.

"We drove for Bernard at Kyalami with Mike Hailwood and Bob Anderson driving the other car. Bernard was a very likeable chap, a very social man. He had lots of money,

Mike Spence in the BRM, South African Grand Prix, 1967. *Stuart Falconer/
David Pearson (www.motoprint.co.za)*

Mike at the Race of Champions event, Brands Hatch, 1967. *Mervyn Silver*

Mike passes the fans at the 1967 Dutch Grand Prix. *Rene Speur*

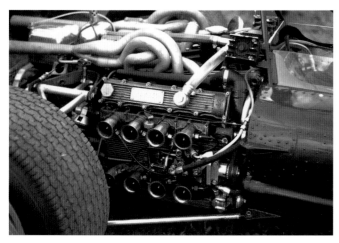

The H16 engine in the BRM. *Mike Spence/Lynne Spence*

Mike at the 1967 German Grand Prix, Nürburgring. *Nils Ruwisch archive*

came from Yorkshire, Richmond way. He was pretty wealthy but I don't think he did much. His brother was the really successful one, with Bernie helping out a bit and Bernie was getting money off that [Author note: Bernard White's brother was Gordon, later Lord White, who ran the Hanson Trust, a successful industrial conglomerate]. He got the bug for racing and Bob Bondurant drove for him for a bit, and then he asked me and Mike to go to South Africa for him for a while. I thought it was just me and Bernie going but then Mike rolled up to drive the GT40 and the Kyalami 9 Hours.

"We had a dreadful mechanic whose name was Bob. I started the race and I had asked him to put it in first gear. Back then we had seatbelts and they were set in a way that they were hanging off the ceiling so that you could get in, harness the seatbelt in and off you go. Well this berk managed to put the gear in reverse! Luckily, I did not reverse it into the wall but obviously it mucked up the start. Then we were doing pretty well after that. We only had the one mechanic, this Bob chap and then Roly Moat joined us – he was the mechanic for Bernie's Formula One car.

"In the end, around Christmas time, Mike Hailwood and I rang Bernie up – I can't remember if Bernie was at the 9-Hour or not – but we did not see him again for a while after that. We were out there for weeks, racing the GT40, and we went to Cape Town and Bulawayo, Lourenço Marques and we were based in Johannesburg. Mike Spence went back to England. We also went down to Pietermaritzburg. We had a good run really. Mike Spence only came for that one race and I did not have much to do with him then.

"I later drove for Bernie at the British Grand Prix in his car and then went to Canada for the Grand Prix and then the Springbok Series. After 1968, I did not see him. He lost interest in racing. He was one of these volatile rich guys who said [Hobbs attempts, with his American-tinged Midlands accent, a thick Yorkshire accent] 'David, racing's really easy, it's just a business after all, if you can be good at t'business, you can be good at t'racing'.

"I said to him, 'Bernie, racing is a very weird, weird sport, it doesn't make sense. Even if you are a successful businessman, it doesn't necessarily mean you will be a successful team owner'. But then he was not anyway. He was always a day late, he employed cheap labour, the cheapest guys he could find, he always made do with one mechanic rather than two and all that sort of stuff. He had money but I don't know if he had *massive* amounts of money. But he was a real character. Then he moved to Spain, to avoid tax I suppose, but when he realised he had to spend some real money, well, he went off to do

Mike signs autographs for the Nürburgring ADAC 1000km race.
Raimund Kommer

something else and went to Spain to flirt with the girls and dip in the Med!

"I drove Bernard's BRM P261 which was a pretty nice car to drive. I liked it and it handled reasonably well but as I say we only had one mechanic who was just a guy out of Yorkshire, and his toolbox was not very big – one hammer, one screwdriver and that was about it, you know.

"We had no technical expert with the team, of course, and I couldn't contribute that much as it was the first Formula One car I ever drove. The big trouble with it though, it was a beautiful little car to drive but it only had a 2.0-litre engine and everyone else had a 3.0-litre engine! In Canada, it went pretty well in the rain until I spun it. Of course in those days, you could get out, push it around, got back in it and carried on again. That obviously cost me a lot of time as up to then I had doing quite well in the rain because being down 60, 70, 90bhp did not make much difference – it was *very* wet, very, very wet – that was the first ever Canadian Grand Prix.

"So it was a nice car, but we had no real back-up, we did not have tons of spare tyres or spare wheels, we had the very, very minimum to get by on. But we came eighth at the British Grand Prix and I beat the likes of Chris Irwin and Richard

Mike in the BRM P83, German Grand Prix 1967. *John Spence*

Attwood and a couple of other guys who it was good to beat, but it was not exactly setting the world on fire. We had fun with Bernie, he was good to be with." Bernard White remained overseas until his death in December 2008.

The 1966 season had been an immense struggle but Mike improved with his commitment in the face of adversity, his development skills at Lotus, and his two fifth place finishes in one of the most uncompetitive cars on the grid. He outscored Peter Arundell, his replacement at Lotus, by three points. Arundell, still affected by his injuries, scored just one World Championship point as his once gloriously promising career ended in a sad way. When Graham Hill moved from BRM to Lotus to replace Arundell, BRM made their move to get Mike into the works team.

BRM had come up with what it felt was a very workable solution to new engine specifications introduced, as mentioned already, at the beginning of 1966, for the movement to 3.0 litre engines. They, like everyone else, took time to develop

new cars and engines accordingly, but actually enjoyed great success at the start of the 1966 season. Jackie Stewart won the first race of the season, at Monaco, in the BRM P261, powered by the P60 V8 engine. Stewart and his team-mate, Graham Hill were doing extremely well at the start of the season and were lying in second (Hill) and third places at the end of the Dutch Grand Prix, the fifth race of the year. BRM was in third place with 19 points with Brabham the man and Brabham the team leading the way with 30 points.

With the introduction of the P83 and, more significantly, the H16 engine, Hill and Stewart only mustered three more points together in the last four races as Jack Brabham eased to his third World Championship victory and John Surtees, Jochen Rindt and Denny Hulme finished ahead of Hill in the standings.

Tony Rudd, in his book *It Was Fun!* gave some background to the H16 engine's development: "We had an excellent two-valve 1.5-litre V8 engine. But up to 3.0 litres meant a double

A colour shot of Mike at the 1967 German Grand Prix. *Sigurd Reilbach*

Mike passes the pits at the 1967 German Grand Prix. *Raimund Kommer*

Mike also had problems in practice for the 1967 German Grand Prix as this photo shows. *John Spence*

Mike comes to a stop at the 1967 German Grand Prix at the Nürburgring.

Sigurd Reilbach

He seems very relaxed about the differential failure!

HP Seufert/John Spence

Mike at a very wet Canadian Grand Prix at Mosport. *Lynne Spence*

The Canadian Grand Prix, 1967. Despite it being August, the rain came heavily. Mike negotiates the wet track. *Gary Magwood*

– a H16 – which was two flat V8s on top of each other. Historical precedent had not really seen success of flat engine cars, nor had it seen success with 16-cylinder engines bar Auto Union's single-camshaft engine of the mid-1930's. We were actually leaning towards a V12 until supply and performance problems with Weslake took play. It meant a change of mind. A two-valve H16 would be built, but so too would be a four-valve V12 and in 1966, the better one would be raced.

"Early on, the H16 couldn't get water from the lower to the upper cylinder heads, but that ended up being the tip of the iceberg. We had broken camshafts, broken rubber belt drivers, broken crankshafts. Later it was discovered that the crankshaft balance weights would fly off if the engine was over-revved. The car therefore was left with great road holding but it was so heavy and sluggish under acceleration."

Doug Nye, in his books *The Story of Lotus* and *Theme Lotus*, revealed that the mechanics got an immediate sense that the engine was not going to be a success. "We knew we had a weight problem when it took six mechanics to lift the H16 engine off the lorry! The engines were put one above the other with crankshafts geared together. The crankcase soon got overstressed due to the complexity and compactness." Lotus used the BRM engine in 1966 as somewhat of a stopgap. Plans were well in place for the Cosworth DFV engine that enjoyed incredible success, but 1966 was too early for this engine. As a result, Lotus struggled, with Jim Clark nowhere near the top. He won just one race with it, the United States Grand Prix.

Although a BRM works drive was, in theory, better than chugging around in the Parnell-BRM, there was a general feeling of frustration, despondency and even anger around the Bourne-based team at the time Mike stepped into the drive. He raced in a H16-powered BRM ten times finishing – somewhat remarkably – in fifth place on five occasions. There were many observers who argued that 1967 was Mike's

finest. Seasoned motorsport writer David Tremayne wrote in *GP Plus* magazine that "Spence showed flair and mechanical sympathy in bringing the guttural monster home when Stewart often retired." Certainly, Mike's mechanical sympathy was never more required than it was in 1967. Malcolm Angood had noticed a change in him and his driving: "From 1966 onwards he became much more confident as he was learning all the time, taking on new challenges all the time, whether it be with Lotus or BRM. He just progressed more and became more and more confident."

Mike was consistent, just ploughed on, never complained and supported as best he could a rapidly frustrated Stewart, who was seeing a once promising career being hamstrung by the poor performance of the car. South Africa, on 2 January, saw no repeat of his heroics the previous year. Qualifying in 13th place, he retired on the 31st lap due to an oil leak.

He then came fifth at the non-championship Race of Champions, and repeated that result at the Belgian Grand Prix, where Jackie Stewart finished second, which was the only time the two works H16-powered BRMs finished together in the points.

The successive French, British and German Grand Prix events all ended in retirement, but the end to the season was masterful. He finished fifth at Italy, Canada and Mexico with all his points finishes coming after he qualified no higher than tenth and on average, he qualified in eleventh place. So, as well as keeping the car going, Mike was still fighting for higher points finishes despite the car's fragility.

But his best performance was probably at the Monaco Grand Prix. Tony Rudd's biography revealed just how good the drive was, despite the relatively lowly sixth place: "Mike couldn't select fifth or sixth gears. On Dunlop 008s which were not the best grip on a slightly oily circuit, Mike looked after his car amazingly well to bring it to the finish, avoiding giving it full throttle pretty much the whole way through with him really only giving it a boost on the Casino Square, where the transmission is subjected to the most pressure. He put full power up the hill, along the sea front and through the chicane. Despite all these issues, he ran only three seconds a lap behind the leaders all the way through. Benefitting from retirements, Mike came home in sixth. It was notable when the race finished how well he'd looked after the tyres. He'd worn, on a circuit that pulverised tyres, 1mm of tread, whereas Graham Hill had worn 3mm and Pedro Rodriguez 4mm of tread."

Mike mentioned back in 1962 to Jim Meikle that he "Enjoyed driving at Monaco the most. Last time at Monza, I felt I could've gone faster if I'd had a good engine. The most challenging are Solitude and Clermont Ferrand – I'd like to go back to Solitude. I know Snetterton and Goodwood pretty well now, but on the Silverstone GP circuit I always feel I ought to be doing better. But Monaco is my favourite, an enjoyable challenge."

When interviewing Sir Jackie Stewart for this book, I had to apologise to him as I was going to talk to him about the worst season of his career, but with the passage of time he had reconciled himself with an utterly miserable season and could now laugh it off. But as he told me and other writers (David Tremayne in 1997 for *Motor Sport* magazine and Doug Nye for his *Saga of British Racing Motors Volume 3* to name just two): "The H16 was a disaster! It did not matter who was in the car, we all did the same speed. Well, Mike was stuck with that poor BRM car. No, the cars weren't as good but there again you make your own bed, as I did by choosing by BRM, which

I hoped would give me the reliability. I was lucky to arrive as Graham Hill's understudy. Jimmy did not share anything with anybody. I remember I asked him things and he would not talk about them. Graham never held back. Jimmy was very shy. By 1967, we [Mike and I] were driving cars that were really not reliable. He was driving the H16. We barely ever finished races! He was a perfect team mate, I really enjoyed being with him as he was a first class person but I think his time at Lotus was spoilt by the presence of Jim.

"I thought it was a good decision for Mike to join me. He was a young man, he was doing well. He was experienced. By then, I was getting very fed up with BRM because of the H16. I don't care who you would have had in the car – even Jimmy – seldom did we finish races. Mike was modest, shy, lovely. Maybe he was not as aggressive as he might have been, but he was a very good driver. I liked him a lot, a gentle man and a gentleman. Maybe too nice to succeed in Formula One.

"As far at the H16 was concerned, I had by that time realised it was a long battle. Its durability was very poor. It was too big, too heavy and losing out badly under acceleration out of all the slow and medium speed corners. The Repco-Brabhams were small, light and agile whereas we were heavy and cumbersome. Every other car had the advantage over us in almost every department."

One thing is clear about Mike from 1965 to a large part of 1967: there was no obvious complaining, and it appeared to all he was happy to race. Not many drivers would have accepted losing a top works drive through no real fault of

Mike in the BRM, Italian Grand Prix, 1967. *John Spence*

Mike and Jackie Stewart polish their goggles. *Lynne Spence*

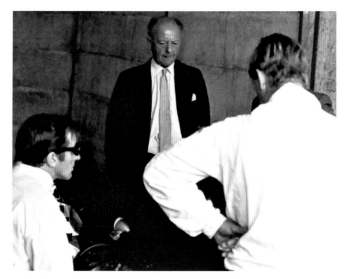

Raymond Mays (centre), the BRM team manager, would have had a worried face for much of 1967. Jackie Stewart (left) and Mike debrief at the 1967 German Grand Prix. *Raimund Kommer*

but Mike did not slow down or get annoyed, he just showed everyone how he could drive when he got the chance. His personality, being easy to get along with and having a good temperament, certainly helped.

Mike's comments about the H16 in *Motor Racing* magazine in December 1967 realistically reflect both loyalty to BRM and Mike's general attitude, but he was politely honest. If Mike had lived to recall the H16 now, the answer would likely be different, but this is what he committed to at the time: "It's a big heavy car to drive, all the controls are heavy, yet it's quite controllable. It has a very nice smooth engine with very good throttle response. The car is possibly a little too heavy but the real problem is that there is just too much weight overall. The engine gives quite good power but it is very peaky, requiring a 6-speed gearbox, and we spend far too much time changing gear.

Tony Rudd with Mike Spence at the US Grand Prix practice at Watkins Glen, 1967. *Rick Braverman*

"Is it a potential winner in 1968? In its present form, definitely not. But it is being further developed and by next year we should see a H16 BRM very near to the weight limit and with considerably more power. This might well turn it into a winner on fast circuits like Spa or Monza, but it may still suffer from poor low speed torque at places like Monaco."

With Stewart's departure to Matra (albeit the cars were run by Ken Tyrrell), Mike was now in a position to lead a works team for the first time in his career. No longer the man in the shadow of a Scottish team leader, he could now influence his own destiny.

The BRM Pits. The white-haired man closest to the camera is long-serving BRM mechanic, Willie Southcott. *Mike Spence/Lynne Spence*

The way it was – no cover from the weather and no fancy pits for the BRM mechanics. *Mike Spence/Lynne Spence*

Maidenhead Memories

"The Mike Spence name stood for quality, we were a known commodity. People wanted to work with us or for us"
Peter Davies, Mike Spence Ltd sales director and friend of Mike

Iain Stowe drives his Lotus Elan BRM (car number six) at Prescott, 2011. *Iain Stowe*

On 11 March 1966, the local newspaper, the *Maidenhead Advertiser*, trumpeted the formation of Mike Spence Ltd, announcing that Mike, when not racing, would demonstrate Lotus and Rover cars at the new showroom at 11 High Street. The business was opened by Sir John Whitmore, the 1965 European Touring Car champion and a good friend of both Mike Spence and David Porter. Local drivers David Good (who had some involvement with the firm), Alan Rees and David Piper all attended the opening ceremony.

The company was founded a month before the opening. Peter Davies was the sales director from the start of the garage and continued for a while after Mike's death. "It was Mike's idea, originally, to start the business. He liked the thought of a specialist garage, maybe linked to Lotus, maybe not. He knew lots of Lotus affiliated companies in and around London. However, due to his racing, he left it to David Porter to implement the majority of the set-up with Mike remaining involved. I joined when I was approached by David. Just before I worked there, I was actually working in Muscat, Oman. I then moved back to the UK and put my CV in to a recruitment agency for garage specialists. David Porter found my CV and cut the middle-man out and approached me directly.

"Mike was not as involved intricately really, other than his name. He was a kind of ambassador if you will. He did support it the very best he could and had an interest in the workshop, but it was largely myself as sales director and David as managing director. However, Mike's benefits were that he had a well-known profile, which naturally reflected on the company and he also had lots of links. He was a grand prix driver with a large following of fans, so that helped, particularly with Lotus."

When Mike was away, which was frequently, Porter and Davies looked after the company. After identifying the need for proper workshops after a temporary set-up at Bell Street, the business opened a workshop and garage in Reform Road, next to Ron Harris Racing, Mike's former team. There are still garages and workshops based in the industrial estate there, so it isn't too difficult to imagine the scenes 50 years ago as a wave of luxurious cars arrived from the showroom just a two-minute drive over Bridge Road.

Mike had his own favourites. In 1962, he told Jim Meikle that "My ideal road car would be a Porsche 2.0-litre Carrera, that's if I had unlimited money of course. I may change this when I get the Lotus Elan." This was some years before Mike and the Elan were forever linked. In 1967, having established himself in sports cars, Formula One and the business world, Mike said to *Motor Racing* magazine that a Porsche was still his favourite. "Being in the business, it can be any car, any day,

Mike Spence Ltd, Maidenhead. **Raymond Thatcher/John Spence**

but my favourite was a Porsche 911S . I like it very much, I like its reliability no matter how hard I drive it. I have tried E-Types and Ferraris, but they are maddening to drive in this country of 70mph limits. I've sold the Porsche now but will try out some other cars."

The Spence garage was most widely associated with the Lotus Elan BRM. This was a special version of the Lotus Elan that Spence and BRM had agreed to modify. The colour scheme was as per the BRM livery of at the time Spence was involved with them, which was a dark green (officially, according to BRM historian Doug Nye, it was called 'dark lustrous green') with a dayglo orange nose band. The engine was modified by BRM in Bourne, with the Spence team making the appropriate modifications when requested by their excited soon-to-be owners.

A sales pamphlet from the time, written by Peter Davies, gives the actual background to what made a Spence Elan as opposed to a Lotus Elan. For posterity and clarification, I've repeated most of it below. Bear in mind this is from 1967 and, as a comparison, £50 in 1967 would be worth around £750 in 2021.

'At the same time as introducing the Lotus Elan BRM, Mike Spence Ltd announce a number of conversions to increase the performance of existing Elans to make these comparable with the Lotus Elan BRM. In short, they are 'Spence Specifications'.

- Gas flowed cylinder head – The cylinder head is removed, stripped and modified and reassembled. .010# is removed from the cylinder head to increase compression ratio. Price including fitting is £50.
- Special camshafts and carburettor settings – Cosworth CPL2 camshafts are fitted. Existing Weber carburettor chokes are changed for 33mm chokes and the main and air correction jets are altered. Price is £40.

- Balancing – Stripping complete engine. The crankshaft, flywheel and clutch are balanced individually and then as a unit. Connecting rods and pistons are accurately matched. The engine is reassembled using a Cosworth modified pressure relief valve and felt filter. Price is £40.
- Exhaust System – A four-branch racing type exhaust manifold and pipe is used in conjunction with either a Jaguar E-Type straight through silencer or an Elan special equipment silencer. Price is £45.
- Large Diameter Inlet Valve – These may be fitted at the same time as gas-flowing the cylinder head for an additional cost of £25.
- BRM Steel Connecting Rods – can be fitted. Price on application.
- Oil Cooling System – A Taurus thermostatically controlled oil cooler is installed. Price £21, fitting £5.
- Special Paint Finish – Your car may be re-cellulosed in any polychromatic finish to choice by our highly skilled ex-Mulliner paint sprayer. Price £65.

That very highly skilled ex-Mulliner (a well-known coach builder in Chiswick that nowadays is the personal commissioning department for Bentley) paint sprayer is a chap called Alan Rigarlsford. Alan worked at Mike Spence Ltd as the bodywork painter for the Elans and all other variety of machinery that passed through the workshop. Even in his 80s, Alan is still working and involved in bodywork repair and painting with his own firm, Specialised Paintwork, which is an approved Lotus body shop. The famous Lotus badge is displayed proudly their office in Calcot, Berkshire. It was at that location, in 2020, that he recalled his relatively brief time in Mike's company.

"Mike was a very quiet, relaxed chap. I'd see him around the workshop. I only knew him for about 18 months before his death and, although he was the figurehead of the company, it was only his name. Other people put money into the company and they were the ones behind it, Mike was just there.

"He was not a businessman in *any* way. A racing driver, yes, a really, really nice person, cracking chap but not a businessman. He never once bothered me. I'd be certainly working away in the workshop and then suddenly I'd look up

SUPPLIED BY

MIKE SPENCE LIMITED

ELAND HOUSE   11 HIGH STREET   MAIDENHEAD   BERKSHIRE
TEL:28539

Mike Spence Ltd sticker. *Alan Rigarlsford*

Lotus Elan BRM Car number six. *Iain Stowe*

and he's standing by the side of me, hands in his pockets just floating around the workshop. He was always out testing, you see. In some weeks we did not see him at all, especially if he was in a race across the world. He would go with Jim Clark, they would stick together and that's how it was really. I would say in the 18 months I saw him 30-odd times."

"His name was above the business, but it was a chap by the name of David Porter who really ran it. David Porter was his mate from years back. Peter Davies was the sales director and he, Mike and Porter were the main people involved in the business for a few years. It was Peter that got me involved in Mike Spence Ltd in the first place. He was working in Farnham Road, Slough, and he was there as a salesman. He served with me in the forces in the Green Jackets infantry regiment and out of the blue one day he came in to where I was working and said 'I am getting a job at Mike Spence in Maidenhead and the cars are coming through due to Mike's association with Lotus'.

"He said that the cars are coming through at an incredible rate. Lotus could not produce the cars quickly enough. The cars came in kit form in those days, and the cars came through very quickly as Lotus had just moved from Cheshunt to Norfolk. Because they had only just moved, they had not got the paintshop ready and, as it was a kit car, the engine (from BRM), wheels and suspension came down completely separately. Peter said to me, 'We have got the first car coming through, could I help with the painting of it?' I helped out but initially worked for my company. After a month, they [Peter and David] said 'This is silly now as we have got too much work and we have got a unit out the back, would you like to join us?' I did about 30 of those in a month and there was an 18-month waiting list. Then it all blew up with Mike's death.

"A couple of other people were involved in the company. There were two who also competed in hillclimbs. One was a chap called David Good and the other was Sir Nicholas

Mike's car and trophies at Mike Spence Ltd. *Raymond Thatcher/John Spence*

Williamson. Good only had one arm, he sat bolt upright and he used the stub of his arm to hold the wheel in place and was rarely beaten. Remarkable really.

"There was no office for Mike at the company – there was one small office in the workshop which David Porter had, and there was one sales office. David Porter ran the workshop. Malcolm Angood was the original mechanic for Mike in Formula Junior and Formula Two. Next door to us was Ron Harris, who had a showroom back in those days, and Malcolm was also involved with him.

"The next thing I knew is that they were going to produce a BRM engine in one of the Lotus Elans. BRM came down with Sir Alfred Owen. An impressive man; sometimes people come in and give the room a different aura immediately. He was one of those chaps, also immaculately turned out. He came to the office and the next thing I knew, we has all these cars coming down. Because it was a kit car, the engine would also now arrive separately from Bourne along with all the other stuff from Lotus. I would finish the cars in BRM

green with the dayglo bumpers. BRM supplied the colours, I produced around eight of them in BRM green. There were only ever eight genuine Elans. Anything that was official was given a BRM stamp. The highest number we've got to with the official stamp that I know of is number six. One is out in New Zealand, one is in the United States of America."

To interject into Alan's memories and to try and clear this up, it appears the actual total is either eight or nine. Peter Davies thinks it was between seven and nine in his conversations with me and, on an internet forum a few years before his death, David Porter went for "No more than ten". Nowadays, as Peter Davies says, "There are thousands of fakes and the nine originals have become hundreds!"

Back to Alan Rigarlsford: "It was a mind-blowing 18 months or so. We had everyone come down to the workshop. *Autosport* did road testing with John Bolster and then gave us a nice write-up and then, subsequently, everyone came to test this little car. We got all sorts of people walking in and out but Mike, if he was there, was always in the background."

Another advertisement, this one in *Motor Sport* in September 1967, summed up the variation the business offered and its little wonder Alan Rigarlsford and his colleagues were so busy. As well as being able to pre-order the Lotus Elan One, other attractions for the discerning Lotus car fan were the Elan-BRMs for £1560, the Elan Drophead and the Fixed Head Coupé for £1299 each, a 8000sq ft workshop service area, bodyshop and paintshop, Elan 5-speed gearbox conversions, a wide range of Elan parts and equipment including wheels and rear axle assemblies and then also tuning and modifications to a wide range of Lotus cars.

"Mike bought a Ferrari once, but he was not really happy with it, it always coughed and spluttered when it went to London so he chucked it in and bought a sand-coloured Porsche. He said that was the bee's knees. He'd put his foot down whenever there were no traffic and coppers around and he just *loved* that car.

"When Mike died, the business ambled along. David Porter and Peter Davies were gutted. Everyone was. Then a chap called Vivian Talfourd-Cook bought the company and David left. Talfourd-Cook renamed the business Mike Spence Developments and they bought the building next door [ex-Ron Harris] and began producing Formula Ford and Formula Three cars [Mike Beckwith was one of the drivers] so the Mike Spence name carried on in racing for a few years, but it was nothing to do with Mike. It was a real shame how it all ended."

Peter Davies: "The Lotus Elan was a very good car. It had the best of both Lotus and BRM involvement with proper engine specification. It was very much a 'pocket rocket'. Now they go for astronomical prices. Just before Mike's death, he was looking to expand. He was looking to move the garage internationally and have a base in a number of countries. He was certainly heavily involved in setting something up in America, where his profile had increased with Chaparral and Can-Am. I was not aware he was setting something specifically up in Australia but, as his parents were out there, I would imagine he would have also set up a garage there. BRM had links to other places, too, which he was speaking to Tony Rudd about.

"I think our greatest achievement at the garage was that we were known, very quickly, and very widely, for our quality. The Mike Spence name stood for quality, we were a known commodity. People wanted to work with us or for us. We were known by customers in America, France, Germany, even the Solomon Isles of all places, for quality."

It's natural to see the Mike Spence name by a racing team and think it was to do with the racing driver but, as it happens, it has no direct link to the man himself. The team ran a number of cars, including a Lotus 47 FVA, a Lotus 23B, a Royale RP4 F100. For Ian Taylor, a local lad who was highly promising in Formula Ford and Formula Three in the early 1970s but never had a real budget to progress to Formula Two, let alone Formula One, the team ran a March 708 in an orange, mauve and white livery. Peter Davies also

LOTUS ELAN "S.S"

MODIFICATIONS TO EXISTING ELANS TO "SPENCE SPECIFICATION"

At the same time as introducing the Lotus Elan B.R.M., Mike Spence Ltd. announce a series of conversions to increase the performance of existing Elans to make them comparable with the Lotus Elan B.R.M.

GAS FLOWED CYLINDER HEAD

The cylinder head is removed, stripped, modified by experts highly skilled in re-work racing Elan heads and re-assembled. .010" is removed from cylinder head to increase compression ratio. Price including fitting .... £50. 0. 0.

SPECIAL CAMSHAFTS & CARBURETTER SETTINGS

Cosworth CPL2 camshafts are fitted. Existing Weber Carburetter chokes are changed for 33 mm. chokes and the main and air correction jets are altered £40. 0. 0.

BALANCING

Stripping complete engine. The crankshaft, flywheel and clutch are balanced individually and then as a unit. Connecting rods and pistons are accurately matched. The engine is re-assembled using a Cosworth modified pressure relief valve and felt filter. £40. 0. 0.

EXHAUST SYSTEM

A four branch racing type exhaust manifold and pipe is used in conjunction with either a Jaguar 'E' type straight through silencer or an Elan special equipment silencer. £45. 0. 0.

LARGE DIAMETER INLET VALVES

These may be fitted at the same time as gas-flowing the cylinder head for an additional cost of £25. 0. 0.

B.R.M. STEEL CONNECTING RODS

Price on application.

OIL COOLING SYSTEM

A 'TAURUS' Thermostatically controlled oil cooler is installed. (Fitting £5 extra) £21. 0. 0.

SPECIAL PAINT FINISH

Your car may be re-cellulosed in any Polychromatic finish to choice by our highly skilled ex-Mulliner paint sprayer. £65. 0. 0.

For further details and road test car please contact Mr. Peter Davies at the sole distributors, Mike Spence Ltd., Eland House, 11 High Street, Maidenhead, Berks. Telephone: 28539.

The Mike Spence Ltd modifications. *Alan Rigarlsford*

Bellavista Cottage, Maidenhead – Mike and Lynne's home for a few years.
Lynne Spence

The Mike Spence name continued after Mike's death but run by totally different management. This is a Mike Spence-entered car for Ted Bundy in the 1969 Clubmans Championship. *Ted Walker*

took part in some rallies in an Escort Twin Cam. But that's as far as I'll really cover that particular aspect of the business, which also opened a location in nearby Henley in Oxfordshire and in Shinfield, near Reading, after Mike's death and moved the head office and most of the operations to the former site. The showroom in the High Street remained for another two decades but nothing now, other than in local people's memories, exists of the Mike Spence name in Maidenhead.

Mike, with Lynne, enjoyed living in Maidenhead as well as basing his business there. The Berkshire town was conveniently placed, too. From his home, Mike was just 14 miles from Heathrow Airport and, although there are better and quicker roads now, he would still have only been about an hour and a half from Silverstone, Goodwood and Brands Hatch.

Malcolm Angood confirmed that accessibility was a key to Mike plumping for Maidenhead. "Mike had a bungalow in Maidenhead when he was racing with Ron Harris, who, of course, was also based in Maidenhead. Mike moved there initially because it was easier to be near Ron and then realised how central the place was to a number of key places. I lived there in the bungalow as I was working on the Formula Two cars. I would continue to see Mike, right up until he died, but obviously it became briefer as he went on to Formula One

and went across the world. However, every time he was back we would catch up and chat about racing. He would come and see me race, he'd go to the race meetings with me as much as he could – the Formula Three meetings and Formula Two. He would not have a break as it were, he was a real enthusiast who did it for the love of the sport and would enjoy watching an event even if he was not racing."

Mike often said that he did not get much time at home but, in an interview with *Motor Racing* magazine in December 1967, mentioned a few things when he did during rare downtime. "I am interested in a wide variety of sports but don't get time to participate in them anymore. I am keen on cricket and golf. I like to listen to music and history interests me a lot. Books, too, but I prefer fact to fiction and most of my reading would be technical; I read things to find things out, not to be entertained."

Mike was very happy in Maidenhead but this was also reciprocated. He brought in a lot of business, profile and a number of jobs for the locals and upon his death, the Mayor of Maidenhead, Councillor Roy Thomas, paid a warm tribute to Mike: "He was one of the town's best celebrities. We have all followed his progress avidly and I still cannot believe that he is dead. Mike was a man who lived for driving. All of Maidenhead will mourn at the news of his untimely death."

The Chaparral High

"I remember being as comfortable around Mike as any driver that
I worked with. Working with him was an enjoyable part of my career"
Jim Hall, Chaparral constructor and racing driver

The BOAC 500 race at Brands Hatch. Mike leads the Ferrari 330 P4 of Jackie Stewart as they lap the David Piper-entered Ferrari 250 LM of Hugh Dibley and Roy Pierpoint (55). *John Adams (Racebears)*

There are times in this biography where I hand over to quote, word for word, the efforts of an author and journalist who has blazed the trail already. The passage that follows is the work of eminent US author and journalist, Pete Lyons, who wrote the below in a small pamphlet like book called *Cars in Profile – The Chaparral 2, 2D and 2F* in 1972.

'The Chaparrals were the most innovative American racing cars. They broke more technological ground and advanced the high-performance sciences faster than any automobiles ever made there. They won races and they lost races but, more importantly, they developed ideas, pioneering new concepts in aerodynamics.'

Jim Hall was a mechanical engineer who raced in sports cars and Formula One before concentrating on developing his sports racers. Hall gained a reputation for developing light, strong and mechanically efficient cars. Backed up by his own oil money and support from General Motors, Hall and his friend and fellow former racer, Hap Sharp, soon gained an outstanding reputation for fast cars with excellent grip. They weren't always the prettiest cars, but they were the most scientifically advanced with Hall continuously trying out new ideas and never settling for second best. A problem would, for Hall, simply be a challenge to continually amend and tweak the car to its optimum performance.

It was a challenge that attracted Hall to form Chaparral. Dick Troutman and Tom Barnes had both been involved with Lance Reventlow's Scarab project, which had enjoyed some success in Californian sports car racing, but a disastrous Formula One effort led to the overall demise of the project. Troutman and Barnes met Hall in 1960 and wanted to build an American sports racing car along the lines of the front engined Scarab, but it needed to be smaller and lighter, with European influences. Initial progress was promising, but it was the Chaparral 2 that gave the outfit the real dominance they strived for.

Graffiti or art? PH is Phil Hill. A pit wall at the Nürburgring, August 1966.
Raimund Kommer

Mike Spence and Hap Sharp, co-founder of Chaparral, before the BOAC 500 race at Brands Hatch. **Peter Darley**

The Chaparral 2 had a modern supple suspension with a fibreglass chassis structure. With fibreglass, the team was able to create and exploit shapes to form smooth transitions at structure junctions, using vacuum pressure to create the structure. This doesn't sound like much today but, to put it into context, let's put it like this; a complete Formula One chassis was not moulded until 1981, nearly 20 years later. Vacuum pressure was rarely seen in any race car shop anywhere for at least another ten years. This was the basis, once everything else came together, for a car that would win race after race.

Chaparral built the 2D to compete in the sports car world championship in 1966, with Phil Hill and Jo Bonnier winning at the Nürburgring. The 2F was built for 1967 with Mike joining Phil Hill.

Spence will forever be associated with the Chaparral 2F, arguably as much as any in his career. He was very much in demand despite – or maybe because – of the drop down from Lotus to Parnell-BRM. An article in the *Montreal Gazette* later in the season revealed that Bruce McLaren wanted Mike to compete in Can-Am if Denny Hulme, Bruce's first choice, could neither commit nor perform well enough in late 1966.

Chaparral was given a choice of building a car to meet the 748kg minimum weight limit to meet the criteria for the world sports car championship or they could choose a lower weight limit of 698kg and run an older aluminium engine. At the start of 1967, Chaparral made the decision, by using revolutionary computer programming, to adopt a 7.0-litre engine, which allowed significantly much more brake horse power with just a mere 38kg weight penalty, which in turn led to a faster car through corners. The bodywork went through an extensive rebuild to generate more downforce and, to balance that, a large aerofoil was mounted onto struts to the back. Significantly, these were not mounted to the body of the car but to the suspension uprights. This aerofoil was connected hydraulically to a foot pedal in such a way that the pressure of a driver's left foot would pivot it nearly flat for minimal drag on straights, but then the release of pressure would then move it into maximum downforce position to stabilise the car when cornering and braking. This device was brilliantly exploited by Phil Hill and Mike Spence.

Despite the 7.0-litre engine, the car was quite light weight. The chassis, one of the revolutionary monocoques created in 1964, was light as always, but the engine was made of alloy and not iron. Even the batteries were lighter than usual as they were made of nickel cadmium, a discovery made by the aerospace world. It's also worth noting that Hall also took inspiration from the surfboarding world in terms of balance. The Chaparral stood out. Every other car in the field looked, to the average person on the street, similar. But not the 2F. Aside from the large aerofoil, it had a different shaped nose and bodywork.

Phil Hill was in the swansong of his racing life and the 2F would be the car he would finish his competitive career in. He was a fan of the car, which is saying something considering the vast amount of machinery Hill raced over the 20 years he competed. As he recalled to Pete Lyons in the aforementioned *Cars In Profile* book: "It was much like any good racing car to drive, only it was a hell of a lot more honest. It had better grip, it was more predictable, it had a lot more downforce than any other car at that time. The wing was fail safe. If I needed to brake with my left foot, then the wing just sent into full drag, full downforce and maximum understeer mode."

Despite all these remarkable technological ideas and prowess, the car suffered from numerous problems, largely due to its gearbox. A new gearbox was not built as it was felt

Phil Hill and Mike Spence share a laugh at the pit wall. *Lynne Spence*

at the time that the existing internal parts could cope with increased torque. This, rather emphatically, proved not to be the case.

Jim Hall recalled to Richard Falconer for his Chaparral book, covering the history of the team in the early 1990s: "You had to have a definite ability to using the gearbox. It took a different skill, which some people were used to and some people were much better than others. It was not important to be gentle with it, but there were certain things you couldn't do. You had to follow the numbers." Troy Rogers, who was the lead fabricator and mechanic for the team was more direct with Falconer: "The only problem with the 2F was the gearbox. It just couldn't take it."

Spence was entered for seven races in 1967 for Chaparral, but it did not get off to the best of starts. At the Daytona 24-Hour race, Hill and Spence qualified second. Four hours into the race, Phil Hill made a rare error, crashing the car and accruing terminal suspension damage. The track had been recently repaired and widened and in places, the asphalt was already breaking apart, allowing a gradual build-up of debris,

Mike at the Nürburgring 1000km, 1967. **Nils Ruwisch archive**

The Chaparral being fuelled at the Nürburgring 1000km, 1967. Mike and Phil Hill sit on the pit wall. **Hemel Hempstead Echo and Post/John Spence**

Mike at the Nurburgring, 1967. *HP Seufert/John Spence*

which was particularly noticeable in areas where the road circuit rejoined the banking. Hill, a veteran of two decades of racing was very upset, but surprisingly spoke out against Mike a little, maybe somewhat to deflect the attention away from his mistake.

Hill said to a few people, including *Motor Sport* magazine: "I just wish Mike Spence had just said something about that, like, 'Watch the marbles going on the banking'. That is all it would have taken. But nobody said anything at all about it. I just sort of went back out there and not even that fast, but it just flew up onto the wall. I had never experienced such chagrin and remorse in my entire career as that. It was terrible, Jim was upset – anyone would be – as we were in the lead."

At the 12 Hours of Sebring race, held around two months after Daytona, Jim Hall stepped in, maybe fortuitously, while Hill stewed over the Daytona calamity. This was not as a result of Hill's mistake but because the 1961 World Champion was hit by acute appendicitis. Once again, the 2F impressed with second place in qualifying. But again, like Daytona, all the combined efforts of Mike and Jim were for naught when the gearbox failed, an early warning sign of what was to come. The 2F had failed to start initially. Spence got it going

but the whole grid had gone around the first turn and he was dead last. He made an incredible comeback, hauling his way up a quite astonishing 40 places in just two laps to put the 2F back among the leaders. When both the leading Ford cars took pit stops, Spence took the lead until transmission failure occurred.

The 1000kg of Monza event was the next race for the 2F, with Mike reunited with Phil Hill again with the 1961 World Champion having recovered sufficiently. Spence qualified in first place but again, while dicing at the front, driveshaft failure ended his chances. The Spa 1000km saw another transmission seal fail, and the Nürburgring 1000km and then Le Mans was the same result – gearbox and/or transmission failure. The really frustrating thing for everyone was that the speed was clearly there as Spence qualified no lower than third for every race that season.

Somewhat ironically, at the Brands Hatch BOAC 500 race, the Chaparral's lowest grid position of the year ended up being converted into its best result. It was the last race of the championship and ended up being the last competitive race of Phil Hill's career. Before the Brands Hatch race, the team went to Mike's garage in Maidenhead and operated from the workshop there for a while.

The BOAC 500 at Brands Hatch. *Peter Darley*

Mike jumps out of the car at the Le Mans 24-Hour for a driver change. *Ted Walker*

The race was one of Mike's most memorable and notable wins and was covered extensively at the time. There are few better scribes of race reporting in motorsport history than Denis Jenkinson and, as such, a truncated review of the race follows below from *Motor Sport* magazine's lead writer at the time along with my narrative.

The race captured the imagination of many at the time, largely because of the wide range of machinery competing. Jackie Stewart, Chris Amon and Paul Hawkins were all in works Ferrari P4s while there were five works Porsches (910 and 907 models) with top drivers such as Jochen Rindt, Graham Hill, Jo Siffert and Bruce McLaren competing in the German manufacturer's machinery. The other drivers included Jack Brabham, David Hobbs, John Surtees and Denny Hulme and sports car specialists such as Richard Attwood, David Piper, Hugh Dibley, Hans Herrmann, Vic Elford, Mauro Bianchi and Brian Redman. With Lola-Chevrolets, many Ford GT40's, Lotus Elans and Lotus 47s and even an Austin-Healey 3000, the grid in terms of both quantity and quality of personnel. The cars resembled something like a modern-day historic festival, but it was all in

Kent at a circuit which was not quite used to the quantity of the large monster-sized works cars.

I'll hand over to 'Jenks' for a short while to describe further: 'The two practice sessions went off happily, with a friendly atmosphere all round. Practice was on Thursday and Friday afternoons, Saturday being clear for preparation for the six-hour event on Sunday. There were the usual things going on during practice, Graham Hill was trying to persuade Porsche to redesign their cars, Stewart was doing the same with the P4 Ferraris, David Piper's LM Ferrari had an electrical short circuit when Hugh Dibley was driving it and it caught fire, David Prophet crashed his Ferrari LM and the Chaparral was proving more suited to the circuit than was expected.'

Denny Hulme set the practice pace in the Lola-Chevrolet with fellow Lola driver John Surtees running a close second and the Spence/Hill car in third place. Over to Denis Jenkinson again: 'The thirty-six cars on the start line made an impressive sight and an even more impressive sound as they got away at twelve noon to start the six-hour race, under a grey sky.'

Another shot of Mike at the 1967 BOAC 500. *John Spence*

Mike on his way to winning the 1967 BOAC 500. *Hemel Hempstead Echo and Post/John Spence*

Mike at the BOAC 500, Brands Hatch, 1967. **Roger Dixon**

'Hulme was a bit slow off the mark, Surtees shot off into the lead and Hawkins nipped in behind him, followed by Scarfiotti, Spence and Hulme. On only the second lap Surtees went into the pits with the red Lola-Chevrolet with the push-on connection to the ignition coil wrongly fitted, which put the car right out of the running. This left Hawkins in the lead in the third of the works Ferraris and for nearly fifteen minutes Hawkins held the lead, but first Hulme got by, then Spence and then Scarfiotti.'

Hulme, the New Zealander, Mike and the Italian veteran Scarfiotti then spent a long portion of the race competing at a frenetic pace out the front, working through the traffic of privateer cars as they came to lap them. As the first of the six hours approached, things worked in Mike's favour. Denny Hulme had to make a pit-stop when a rocker arm broke on the engine, and then Scarfiotti lost control and spun but made it back to the pits for the first of the driver change-overs. Mike was now leading the Ferraris of Stewart and Scarfiotti and the Porsche of Jo Siffert and maintained that lead until an hour and a half into the race when Phil Hill took over when the car was being refuelled.

It was not all plain sailing for Hill and Spence though. Shortly after the two-hour mark, one of the Firestone tyres had a puncture and Hill lost a place to Chris Amon in the Ferrari. Phil Hill got past in due course and was leading by the third hour, when Mike and Phil swapped over again.

Stewart, who had swapped with Amon earlier in the race, was right behind and soon retook first place, starting to stretch his lead slightly. It was not for about another hour that the Chaparral took the lead again.

Over to Denis Jenkinson again: 'With one hour to go the Chaparral (Hill) led by eighteen seconds from the Ferrari (Amon), which was in turn a lap and a half in front of the first Porsche (Siffert), but the Ferrari had one more fuel stop to make. This was good for the Chaparral, and anyway Phil Hill was comfortably increasing his lead. With only ten minutes left to run, the second place Ferrari screamed into the pits for a quick refill and for Stewart to take it through to the finish. It was as smooth and slick a pit-stop as anyone could wish for. Stewart was away and barely a minute had been lost, so second place was safe, but equally it meant that the Chaparral was now firmly heading for a well-deserved victory.

'After six hours of fast and furious racing, the first two cars finished on the same lap, having covered 211 laps of the twisty little circuit. It had been as fine a long-distance race as we have seen this season and certainly the best in England for many a year. The Chaparral victory was loudly applauded and it was a pity that Jim Hall was not there to see it, but his partner Hap Sharp was in charge and the handful of mechanics who have been working on the cars in Europe all this season were more than satisfied.'

Troy Rogers, the team's fabricator and mechanic, later recalled to Richard Falconer for his Chaparral book that "Brands Hatch was my favourite victory. That was good, in that Spence was at home and we thought an awful lot of Mike."

This, on balance, has to be seen as Mike's most notable win. The victory at the South African Grand Prix was, to be honest, through luck and Jack Brabham's retirement, although of course any driver has to put themselves in a position to benefit from the misfortune of others. The Race of Champions win was deserved, but again it needed the combined misfortune to hit Dan Gurney and Jim Clark. Although Phil Hill takes a good share of the credit, this drive was down to fast, consistent and skilful driving with expert race management to negotiate the back markers. This was very much down to Mike's rapidly growing confidence.

This race was the perfect way for Phil Hill to bow out at the top. As he later told *Motor Sport* magazine, he had already contemplated retirement some while before Brands; "The telephone rang all the time with people wanting me to drive this and drive that and the other. After Brands Hatch ended that 1967 season, I was not sure if Jim Hall would call me or not. My attitude was now, however, one of take it or leave it. As far as I was concerned, it all faded away. It did not break my heart as my heart just was not really in it. I wish I had started F1 in 1956. I wish I had been able to drive the Chaparral when the motivation and my career was not in such a state of decay. It was already detrimental somewhat and if I had carried on, I was just going to be disenchanted later."

Phil Hill had the very rare (if not unique) distinction of winning his first ever race and his last one. Eighteen years earlier on 24 July 1949, he won a three-lap event at Carrell Speedway in a MG. Hill then built up a classic car restoration business, remaining involved for 25 years. He later also commentated, wrote articles for *Road & Track* magazine, and

What most competitors saw that day – the Chaparral leading in the distance. *Peter Darley*

became a regular visitor to historic events. Son Derek later raced but had to retire when Parkinson's Disease took a toll on his father. Despite illness, Phil continued to visit historic events right up to just before his death on 28 August 2008.

Mike's most extensive feedback about Chaparral came in *Motor Racing* magazine in December 1967: "Of all the cars I've raced in the Chaparral is my favourite. It's a great car and I have thoroughly enjoyed driving it, especially with Phil Hill as a team-mate." When asked what it was like to drive, Mike replied: "It requires a completely different technique. For a start, there's no clutch, just a brake pedal on the left and another for the spoiler, and then the throttle on the right. The automatic is a very good thing for long-distance Group 6 racing; it definitely takes a great deal of the fatigue out of a 24-hour race.

"The whole car is very nice to drive, very easy and very precise. It does everything well in all departments and as a whole, it is a very well designed racing car. The spoiler is activated by the pedal and, to trim it on the straight, you press the pedal and then when you come to a corner, you simply lift off and it automatically returns to the spoil position. It does not have much effect on a tight circuit like Brands, of course, it is meant more for places like Le Mans and Spa. If you had the same kind of set up on a grand prix car, I think the automatic transmission would work, but only if it were possible to design an automatic unit as light as an ordinary gearbox. But it would have to be designed to make best use of the engine's power band, which on a Formula 1 car is pretty limited. But I feel sure that the future will bring many new developments in the aerodynamic field."

"Mike was absolutely in his prime with the 2F," Phil Hill said to David Tremayne for *Motor Sport* magazine: "I had the greatest respect for him as a driver and as a man."

Franz Weis, an immigrant from Germany who worked as a mechanic with Chaparral from the very early days, remembered Mike to Richard Falconer for his Chaparral

A very happy Mike Spence and Phil Hill after the BOAC 500. *Peter Darley*

Mike did testing of the Chaparral in the US and this shot is from his private collection. **Mike Spence/Lynne Spence**

Mike and Phil enjoy the applause from the fans after winning the BOAC 500, 1967. It would be Phil Hill's last race. **Keith Booker**

book: "Mike was nice, very nice. He was a quiet person, but quicker than hell. He really stood on the gas. A really first class driver. I don't think he ever really got the credit he should have. I think he was better than the press made him out to be. The job he did for Chaparral was tremendous. The guy treated everyone equally. He did not think he was better than us, and that meant a lot to the mechanics."

Before we go to the man behind Chaparral and his memories, Jim Hall probably would have continued in 1968, but the FIA limited the engine size of sports prototypes from 7.0 litres to 5.0 litres. Mike confirmed as such to *Motor Racing* magazine in December 1967. "I would very much like to continue with Chaparral but due to changes in regulation by the FIA, they're not building a car for Europe. Jim is concentrating on Group 7 racing in America and I certainly hope to drive for him in next year's Can-Am series".

But in a rare public moment of pique, Mike's annoyance shone through with the decision; "I think it is complete and utter nonsense that a few elderly members of the FIA can make so partisan a decision and change the whole course of a racing formula at six months' notice. They are completely ignoring the best interests of the people most directly involved."

Hall later revealed: "I enjoyed building the car. I enjoyed the 2F, which I thought was a nice car. It was fun to compete against Ford at that time. It was a land of David and Goliath, which was fun, but it was a good challenge. If the 7 litre ban hadn't happened, I think we would have liked to gone on with endurance racing as I believe the 2F was a considerably better car than the Ford MkIV. I think we would have continued at least another year." Chaparral did in fact continue in Can-Am for a little while until 1970, but never took another win after the BOAC race. It's also worth mentioning that Spence would have driven for Chaparral in Can-Am in 1968 had he lived, having just signed a contract weeks before his death.

One year later, Jim Hall revealed to the *Chicago Tribune* that he was offered a drive replacing the now deceased Spence

in the STP turbine car, a drive that eventually went to Joe Leonard. Hall's response was "Spence was a very good friend of mine and I did not have the heart for it."

Jim Hall still lives in Texas and is now in his mid-80s. He is rightly feted for his stunning achievements as a constructor but this often overshadows how good a sports car driver he was, as he took two consecutive United Road Racing Championships in 1964 and 1965 and he won the Sebring 12 Hours in 1965. Hall had wound down his own driving somewhat but a serious crash at Las Vegas in 1968, through no fault of his own, left him with serious knee injuries.

He left the sport for some years after designing a revolutionary fan car (the 2J) which would have probably swept all before it in Can-Am has it not been banned after protests from a number of teams who were more than likely fearful of how little chance they had to win. He returned as a team manager, initially in conjunction with Carl Haas and then later by himself in Formula 5000, Can-Am and Indycar.

The following is a mixture of what he relayed to me and also to Gordon Kirby and Paul Fearnley for *Motor Sport* magazine: "I really thought a lot of Mike. He was likeable, a really good guy. I liked his personality, I liked his driving style and he had a lot of ability. He was a good guy. Sandy and I both liked Lynne. Her sister Gaile was married to Tony Maggs and they, along with Bruce and Patty McLaren, were our closest friends during my time in Formula One in 1963. We all got along well. It was a good group that really helped make our time in Formula One more enjoyable.

"I remember being as comfortable around Mike as any driver that I worked with. I had a lot of confidence in him. He was quick, and I knew he was capable of conserving the car to the end of the race. That's an important part of endurance racing. Drivers need to have enough knowledge about the mechanics of how cars work so they do not make the kind mistakes that some guys that don't have that knowhow sometimes make.

"He gave us exactly what we needed, he was quick and did not damage the car. He was better than I expected. I thought he was confident, professional and comfortable with the car from the outset. Phil was vocal about a few things he did not like about the car, but if Mike had any complaints, he did not make them to me.

"He was an awfully talented driver, he was a smart guy who worked hard. It takes the right kind of person to be on your team who fits in with your people and how they work, and Mike fitted us well.

"I drove a Chaparral 2F with Mike at Sebring in 1967 because Phil, if you remember, had acute appendicitis while we were there and disappeared. It was lucky that I had driven a few laps in practice to work out a handling problem, so I was eligible to race. It was interesting to compare Mike's comments with my own thoughts about the car and compare how we each drove it. I thoroughly enjoyed working with Mike. Working with him was an enjoyable part of my career."

Mike then rounded up the year by competing in Can-Am for the first time, the North American based sports car series which was gaining great popularity and traction across the world as well as America. Mike joined the Ecurie Soucy racing team to drive the McLaren Elva M1B (also sometimes called the McLaren Elva MkII) in five races.

The M1B became available in 1965 and was a very popular car, largely due to their durability. It was created as a response to new regulations brought in that year that, in basic terms, meant the sports cars no longer had to resemble road cars. The M1B saw its spare tyre and luggage compartment removed and large wheels and rear-end downforce added. The car became the first McLaren sports car to undergo wind tunnel testing and significant aerodynamic development, but also had a much stronger suspension than before.

Ecurie Soucy was founded by Canadian millionaire Eustache Soucy, who amassed his fortune through his General Motors dealership. He was based in Rimouski, Quebec,

and the team had enjoyed success with Ross de St Croix earlier that year, with Ross winning the Canadian Can-Am Championship. However, for the American based Can-Am events, Soucy wanted the best driver available. With Spence's stock high through his Chaparral exploits, Soucy made a beeline for Mike.

Gary Magwood is now well-known in Canadian motorsport for two distinctive achievements. Firstly, he founded one of the first Canadian racing schools, developing and increasing his portfolio of schools over time. Secondly, in 1993, he was a co-founder of the Canadian Motorsport Hall of Fame. Twenty-six years later, he was himself inducted in the Hall of Fame he helped create. Before that, Magwood was a racing driver in sports cars and single-seaters but, in 1967, he took part in a very different role as he takes up the mantle and explains: "Eustache Soucy was a car dealer from Quebec. He was only five foot and one or two inches tall and he was a stroppy fucker. He bought the McLaren M1B which was the ex-Chris Amon car which Ross de St Croix drove. Soucy wanted more. He had two French-Canadian mechanics who did not speak a word of English and so he needed an intermediary, so that whoever came to drive the car – in this case Mike – could converse properly with the mechanics and vice versa. Well, that intermediary was me!

"I had been racing in the same Canadian series which stretched all across the vast country and our country is very vast! Soucy bought a *huge* motorhome to go racing. Back then, of course, hardly anyone had motorhomes at all, let alone a large one. It was a home-cum-transporter with a horsebox type trailer at the back. When we first drove it into the paddock, everyone looked around and thought 'What's going on here?'

"Mike was really impressive with the set-up of the car. He knew what he wanted and how to improve it, I learnt from him as I was so impressed. He would come in and say 'I want an extra degree of camber on the left front'

Mike testing the Chaparral. *Mike Spence/Lynne Spence*

Mike didn't race the Chaparral at Las Vegas in the Can-Am championship in 1967, but he couldn't resist a photo of it. To the right of the shot is the Lola of John Surtees. *Mike Spence/Lynne Spence*

Mike's Ecurie Souchy entered McLaren Elva M1B. *Mike Spence/Lynne Spence*

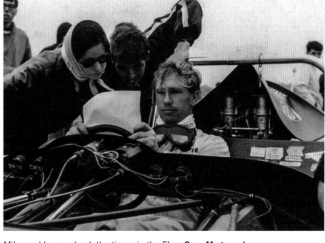

Mike and Lynne check the times in the Elva. *Gary Magwood*

or something like that. Then he would go out and take full advantage of that change. If the car had not been unreliable for a few races, who knows how well he would have done.

"Mike was very quiet, retiring and nice. I would have liked to have worked with him more but unfortunately I got fired. I was driving the motorhome around some twisty-turny roads one time and loved it. The two French-Canadian mechanics were apoplectic thinking they were going to die. So as soon as they could, they ratted to Soucy and I was fired so I did not do all five races with Mike.

"But one story I'd like to tell is the day we were in the diner. It was myself, Mike and Lynne. Some brash guy came up and quite loudly said to me. 'Gee, that Mike Spence you're working with. I am a real fan. What's he like?' I replied, 'Well, he's a very good driver.' This guy goes on a bit wanting to know as much about Mike as he could as he was such a big fan of him. I eventually said to him, 'Look, why don't you come by a little later on and see the car and have a look?' This guy goes away very happily.

"Mike, who was sitting next to me this whole time, taking this all in, leant over and said 'Thank you.' I replied 'What for?' Mike said, 'For not telling that guy that I'm Mike Spence!' Mike was very polite but quite shy but found it very amusing that his alleged biggest fan was across the table from him and did not recognise him!"

Mike's time with the team was overall a positive one, with two third-places finishes at Mosport and Las Vegas, one fifth-place and two retirements. *Autoweek* magazine referred to his race at Las Vegas as "another of a series of literally magnificent drives." As for Eustache Soucy, he died, in Magwood's words, 'in penury on a park bench.'

At the end of 1967, *Motor Racing* magazine published an extensive interview with Mike for its Twenty Questions feature. One of the questions was on the McLaren versus the Chaparral. "First of all, the car I have been driving is a two-year-old design. It's not fair to compare it with this year's Chaparral. It is very simple and unsophisticated and it feels that way to drive. It is an easy, controllable, nippy little car and on a short course where maximum speed is limited, it is still very competitive."

Mike was also asked about Can-Am generally and responded: "Can-Am is a very well organised and very efficient series but I have found the flag marshalling not up to British standards – the highest in my opinion. We've all found difficulty in passing back markers now and then."

The very first question of the Twenty Questions was on Mike's drive for the 1968 season. "I just don't know for certain yet. I would like it to be BRM again and it probably will be. The works will have both 16s and 12s available, using one or the other according to the kind of circuit."

Formula One was Mike's preferred end destination: "It is the ultimate in motor racing. It's the premier formula and the most demanding and satisfying." He used the same interview in *Motor Racing* to angle for a Formula Two drive. "I have not driven in the series because I just haven't had a competitive car to drive yet. I did three races in a Parnell specially modified Lotus 25 but it was not quick enough."

Mike's sports car prowess was obvious but he also admitted "I do not like long-distance races at all. I like to sleep at night! They are much more dangerous than a grand prix owing to the wide variation in speeds of different cars. And the very fact the races are long-distance means that driver are often tired and not so vigilant as they should be. On the other hand, of course, a race like Le Mans is very satisfying to finish."

Unfortunately, the majority of plans Mike had for 1968 never came to fruition.

1968:
A Tumultuous Year

My philosophy with racing is just to enjoy it. I haven't any deep-
seated basic need to be a racing driver, I just like doing it"
Mike Spence, 1967

Mike in the BRM at the Brands Hatch Race of Champions, 1968. *Roger Dixon*

The 1968 season saw some fabulous racing, but April and May in particular was brutal for motorsport, and especially so for British motorsport. Of course, 1968, in isolation, was similar to most years of racing from the early days of the Indianapolis 500 to, I suppose, the late 1990s. Death was pretty much everywhere.

Jim Clark's death on 7 April 1968, was of course, a game changer for Formula One. The leading driver and its figurehead gone in an inconsequential Formula Two race was just the start of a brutal few months. A few weeks later, another of Britain's rising stars, Chris Irwin, saw his career end when he suffered catastrophic head injuries in a practice crash at the Nürburgring 1000km. Two months later, Ludovico Scarfiotti, the 1963 Le Mans and 1966 Italian Grand Prix winner, died in a hillclimb in Germany. Two days later, Ronnie Duman, one of America's top midget and sprint drivers was killed in the Rex Mays 150 race. One month after that, Jo Schlesser, a popular veteran French driver, was killed in a horrific fireball when his experimental Honda crashed early on in the French Grand Prix. Three weeks later, young Chris Lambert, a promising Formula Two driver died in a crash at Zandvoort. There are many other years you can describe such a harrowing roll-call (1958 and 1970 being just two that immediately come to mind), but it seemed that death in the sport was just one of those potential occupational hazards to accept as a consequence of choosing to race.

Mike was quite vocal about his dislike of racing in the rain. He told Jim Meikle: "I do have off days, especially when the weather's inclement. I do not like driving in the wet or when I know I am tired." This stayed with Mike the whole way through his career as he also mentioned this to *Motor Racing* magazine in 1967. "I don't have a favourite circuit, I like the ones where it does not rain best! The circuit I like the least

Chris Irwin (left) and Tim Parnell at the 9 Hours of Kyalami, November 1967. Irwin would be badly injured just a short time after Mike's death.
Mike Spence/Lynne Spence

is Spa Francorchamps in the rain. A really frightening thing about racing is aquaplaning in the wet when you just lose control." Otherwise, as with so many of his era, he rarely mentioned safety.

As Malcolm Angood pointed out, Mike was not one to dwell on stuff anyway. "Mike never talked about the past. He was always looking forward to the future. As an aside, his family were absolutely straight, fantastic people. I would often go back late after working in the workshop, or occasionally at a race meeting and I would sleep at Mike's, and there were never any problems whatsoever. They would always make things easier. They wanted everyone to have a good life and it was great. Mike pretty much took me under his wing. I suppose I was capable at what I did, but his family were always supportive and heavily involved in CERT."

There was a lot for Mike to look forward to in 1968 but he had one last race with the old car and engine. The H16 saw its last grand prix in Mike's hands at the first race of the year in South Africa, which ended up being the final grand prix both Mike and Jim Clark would compete in. He qualified in thirteenth with his new team-mate, Mexican Pedro Rodriguez in tenth, however Pedro was in the new car with the new engine, so Mike's qualification of only one second behind was more than satisfactory, even if being in the older car might have well been galling, considering he had raced with the team already. The fuel system failed after just seven laps and although nobody knew it at the time, Mike had competed in the last of his 36 grands prix.

The BRM P126 was introduced for the full 1968 season with a vastly improved – and lighter – V12 BRM engine. Designed by former Lotus engineer Len Terry, the car did not see a huge amount of success in the time it raced between 1968 and 1969, but Mike's death robbed the team of his development skills to push the car further. But it was more reliable and generally more consistent. Two other closely related models, the P133 and P138, were also introduced.

Mike enjoys the champagne. *Lynne Spence*

W Alec Osborn MBE worked predominantly on the H16 and V12 engines during his time at BRM. He recalls that the P126 was very much a potentially blossoming project: "I worked closely with Mike Spence from the end of September 1967 right up to his tragic death in May 1968. Our task in hand was to upgrade the design and then develop the P126 and P133 cars into competitive machinery through an extensive test programme. This was mainly at Silverstone but also at Kyalami. This would also include his two non-championship races in March and April 1968. The dark days that followed in Madrid were for not just what we had lost but what else could have been achieved."

Richard Attwood, who effectively stepped in for Mike; "The P126 was a nicely balanced car but, as 1968 proved, it did not win a grand prix. Unfortunately, the V12 engine was up against the DFV engine which was outstanding and the benchmark. It did rather well for a long time too. I found out when l drove Jochen Rindt's car at Monaco in 1969 [for Team Lotus as Rindt had been injured in a crash at the previous race at the Spanish Grand Prix], the engine was night and day different to what BRM had at that time."

Len Terry later revealed to Paul Fearnley for *Motor Sport* magazine that: "Mike got to grips with the P126 straight away. He was very impressed with it and reckoned the only thing it lacked was another 20 horsepower."

Mike's first race with the P126 was the non-championship Race of Champions event held at Brands Hatch in March. Spence qualified second, and ran second to winner Bruce McLaren until persistent bottoming (where the suspension scrapes along bumps on the track) wore away an oil line. However, on the Friday, Mike was consistently fastest for most of the day. The quickest person on Friday morning practice received one hundred bottles of champagne and Mike was the quickest man.

The manufacturer of the one hundred bottles was Lanson, which more recently, has been the champagne of choice at the Wimbledon tennis tournament for some 25 years and the company, which can trace its origin back to 1760, is also one of the oldest holders of the Royal Warrant.

Mike in the pits at the 1968 Race of Champions event. *John Spence*

Lanson Champagne, even now, sells around £20 to £25 a bottle so it was either a nice little future nest egg or a wonderful gift for a special occasion. Mike and Lynne enjoyed a tiny bit but, except for really special occasions, neither Mike nor Lynne would drink alcohol. Many were given away as a thank you, most of which Mike gifted to the mechanics, but due to Mike's death just two months afterwards, there were still dozens of the bottles of champagne left over.

After Mike's death, Lynne shipped the remainder of the bottles back to South Africa and kept them for a special occasion, which happened to be the birth of Lynne and her second husband's oldest child. Lynne and her husband David employed a maid at their home who did all the normal household duties. Lynne went to get the bottles, but was in for a surprise. "I had not touched the bottles. We felt the time and the occasion was right when our first child arrived to open a number of the bottles. I went to get one from the attic and imagine my surprise when I saw it was filled up with tea! I then checked all the others – there must have been around fifty or so – all now containing tea! Eventually, it was revealed that our maid had drunk almost every bottle and realising we would notice if it was completely empty had replaced the contents with something else. It took her roughly three years to get through the lot. Realising the bottles were not diminishing as I do not drink alcohol, she felt emboldened and just carried on."

The next race on the cards was the BOAC 500 at Brands Hatch. Held on 7 April 1968, the event, like any other that day, was overshadowed by the news of the death of Jim Clark, who had lost his life at a Formula Two race at Hockenheim in Germany. It affected everyone in the sport in different ways. David Hobbs revealed a little bit more to me what Mike might have been feeling privately: "The most time I spent with Mike was unfortunately at Jimmy Clark's funeral. He

Mike locks up at the 1968 Race of Champions at Brands Hatch. *John Spence*

Mike at the Race of Champions event, Brands Hatch, 1968. *Roger Dixon*

and I were there together, sitting at the back and it was a very emotional thing because everyone was there who wanted to be a racing driver and then you realised the enormity of what had happened. If Jimmy Clark could get killed then I suppose anybody could. You always consider yourself completely bullet-proof and then the odd thing happens like that and maybe not so much."

"Mike and I spent a very emotional 20 minutes on the steps after the funeral commiserating with one another and then of course Colin sent Mike to Indianapolis instead of Jimmy. So just about two weeks later, I was at Mike Spence's funeral. I certainly did not feel bullet-proof anymore."

The car Mike would race at Brands Hatch was the Ford F3L prototype, joining up again with Alan Mann. Alan Mann would later reveal to Paul Fearnley for *Motor Sport* magazine that "Before he drove for me I'd been dismissive of Mike. When it became clear that Jim Clark and Graham Hill weren't available to us for Brands because they had the Hockenheim Formula Two race instead, Mike looked like a safe bet more than anything else, which is why I chose him ahead of Denny Hulme and Jochen Rindt to join Bruce McLaren.

"But he shook the life out of me. He was much more confident than I'd expected. He was quick and very good on the technical side. Frank Gardner and Jack Brabham had driven the F3L and not liked it – they just said it did not feel right, that maybe its wheelbase was too short. After four laps of Goodwood, Mike came in and said he thought the rack was loose. He was right! Its mountings were flexing. He then asked for four or five inches of rear spoiler addition and promptly found another two seconds."

Tony Dron, who collaborated with Alan Mann on a book about his life, *Alan Mann – A Life of Chance*, added to this when

I spoke about Mike to him: "Mike was the only one – not Surtees, not even the great Jack Brabham – that solved this issue with the wheelbase. He came in, showed Alan how the wheel turned and twisted it and then explained thoroughly how to fix it. So, he both visually and verbally helped Alan with that. He was such a great achiever with overcoming technical issues like that."

Mike drove the F3L and was very enthusiastic, but also realistic, about it. In an interview to the *Coventry Evening Telegraph* he said: "I am honoured to have the chance to drive this very exciting new car. It would be marvellous to repeat last year's performance [a BOAC win at Brands] first time out, but perhaps that is asking too much of a brand new car."

The F3L was designed by Len Bailey, a British design engineer who had been employed by Ford, variously at its American base in Dearborn, Michigan, or in Surrey, England, for about a decade. He had worked on the Ford turbine cars and the Mustang road car before working on sports cars, including the GT40. He was commissioned by Alan Mann Racing to build a car around Ford's brand new 3.0-litre DFV V8 Formula one engine.

The F3L was a beautiful car with a low roofline and with appealing aerodynamically efficient curves but, although quick, it suffered from poor stability and chronic unreliability. John Surtees and Jack Brabham were not keen on the instability at high speed and chose not to race it. In due course, rear spoilers were added to stabilise the car.

In the race itself, the completely untested car proved how quick it could be. Bruce McLaren managed to qualify second on the grid. However, Mike's car (he was supposed to be racing with Jochen Rindt) suffered an engine mount failure in practice and did not qualify. Mann, basing his choice on

A great race finished with great disappointment when a driveshaft failed on lap 66. Mike walks across to the pits. *Ian Wagstaff*

Mike's feedback thus far and his reputation as a Brands Hatch specialist, was put into the lead car instead of Rindt. He led the race until a rubber joint in the transmission failed. As with the BRM P126, the F3L would probably have only got better in Mike's hands had he lived. Along with unreliability, there was tragedy for the team. Chris Irwin, Mike's friend, was chosen to drive the F3L at the Nürburgring 1000km race after Mike's death at Indianapolis. Irwin, who had shown immense promise with his Formula One drives thus far, had a massive accident during practice. He survived, but only just, suffering terrible head injuries which would have an effect on him for the rest of his life, and end his racing career there and then.

Mike's very last race was on 25 April 1968 at Silverstone for the *Daily Express* International Trophy in the BRM. Before the race started, there was a one minute's silence for Jim Clark with a lone Scottish bagpiper playing the tune of Crimond (most commonly known as the tune used for the hymn 'The Lord is my Shepherd'), which was not just an appropriate tune but Crimond, in Aberdeenshire, was where Clark had one of his very first races in the 1950s. The immaculately honoured minute's silence was broken by an announcement of 'Gentlemen, start your engines,' and the cavalcade of noise erupted around the Northamptonshire airfield. All, that was, bar the engine of Spence's BRM, but after another attempt, the engine got going.

Mike and Tony Rudd (back to the camera) talk about the BRM away from the track. *Mark Lowrie*

Mike in the Alan Mann Ford F3L at the 1968 BOAC 500. *Roger Dixon*

Mike at the BOAC 500, Brands Hatch, 1968 in the Alan Mann Ford F3L. **Roger Dixon**

Spence harried McLaren at the start with Graham Hill, Jacky Ickx, Hulme and Pedro Rodriguez all together. After being displaced by Hulme, Spence piled on the pressure and produced lap upon consistent lap to take the lead. Lap four may well have been one of Mike's very best of all time when he bravely and confidently passed Hulme and McLaren. Spence's passing moves were notably adventurous, especially when he took McLaren round the outside at Woodcote. Mike also survived a scare when Graham Hill, who had only just got past Mike at Hangar Straight, saw his engine cut out at Stowe and was unable to stop and drifted sideways, narrowly missing Mike's car by inches. He was still chasing Hulme when the engine broke (to be more precise, a timing chain failed) at Club Corner after 40 laps. Once again, Mike seemed a different driver; at the top of his game, more adventurous, quicker and more consistently fast over multiple laps. It ended up being the fastest road race ever run in Great Britain at the time, with eventual winner Denny Hulme averaged 122.17mph over 52 laps.

Richard Attwood: "I remember seeing him driving the P126 at Silverstone in the International Trophy race and actually seeing him undertake Bruce McLaren going into Copse corner! It was a sensational move which was commented on at the time by the public address system."

Tony Rudd, in his book *It was Fun!* saw the benefit of a little pep-talk he had with Mike. "Mike just needed encouraging. He was dependable. At the Brands race he chased Bruce McLaren hard. I said to him 'You are a better driver than he is, the car is as good as his, get in front and stay there.' And he did, before the car broke."

Mike may have been at his most confident, but at least publicly, he was playing it down a little bit. In an article in early 1968, he said in a newspaper interview: "I am halfway up the Formula One scale but not at all in the top bracket." Mike continued racing as he simply loved the sport. When asked by *Motor Racing* magazine in December 1967 for his philosophy about racing, Mike replied: "My philosophy is to enjoy it. I certainly haven't any deep-seated basic need to be a racing driver, I just like doing it. I am also very interested in the technical side of racing."

All of this confidence and enjoyment effectively meant the time was right for possibly his biggest break of his career: a works drive in the Lotus turbine car at the Indianapolis 500 replacing his friend Jim Clark. But it all went horribly, horribly wrong.

Indianapolis: 7 May 1968

"It is a seldom that a rookie comes along and then, straight out of the box, starts running faster than the veterans. That's not to say that there have not been precocious first-time drivers, but it is doubtful if any man seemed to take to the Speedway quite as fast as Spence did"
Indianapolis Star, 1968

Mike and Colin Chapman (left) converse at the practice for the Indianapolis 500, 1968. Dick Scammell, Lotus long-time mechanic, is to the right.

Indianapolis Motor Speedway

Although Mike died as he was coming into his highest trajectory as a driver, he may not have actually carried on racing for much longer had he lived. In October 1965, in an interview with the *Reading Evening Post*, Mike revealed a long-term plan for retirement with words which now carry extra poignancy: "I think it's likely that I shall be retiring from motor racing in two years time, perhaps more. My parents have retired to Australia and we [Mike and Lynne] might well go and live over there with them."

The long-term plan to move to Australia was confirmed again in the 1967 Shell Motorsport profile on Mike, this time by David Porter: "I try to look after the car business so Mike can devote himself to racing. It is probably rather early to be talking about retirement. Nevertheless, he is aware he cannot go on forever. His parents emigrated to Australia a few years ago, where they are now farming. When the time comes, it seems possible he may go out there and join them."

By April 1968, it looked like the plans had changed and, having married, thoroughly settled in Maidenhead and worked on establishing his business, as well as increased success as a driver, it would have seemed that Mike would have continued in the sport for a good few years at least.

However, Lynne revealed this was not the intention. They were planning to plant macadamia trees in Australia as the nuts were expensive and much sought-after. With a lot of hard work and his family around him, Lynne felt Mike would be happy in a far more sedate life. There was a possibility Mike might have stopped earlier, but there was a drought in 1967 which meant pretty much nothing grew and so things were shelved for a little longer.

"Moving to Australia and retiring there was definitely his plan, so 1968 would have been his last year of racing but yes, we were going to go to Nobby's Creek. He might have gone on a little bit longer but I think he would have stopped at the end of the season. There was a new team-mate called Pedro Rodriguez who would not even say good morning to him or to anyone really. Pedro came in, officially as the number two driver, Mike thought 'Wow, I am the number one driver. I don't need to hold back any more, I don't need to support anyone any more, I can go'."

"But Pedro wanted to come in as number one, have the best car, have the best this and the best that and that hurt Mike, I think, personally and I think 1968 would have been his last year.

"But I never encouraged Mike to stop. Never asked him. Stopping him was never discussed. I never said 'Please give up motor racing'. I knew what I was marrying into. Yes, there were a few moments, when you thought 'oh gosh he could get hurt'.

"The times you thought that the most were when you were doing the lap timing, which a lot of the racing wives did. You would be timing and you thought roughly 'OK, he should be around about now,' and when he was not, you would crane your neck and try and see if he was there and then you would worry. You'd try to see the helmet, that's how you noticed them as they all had distinctive helmets. You'd see the helmets first before the number. He always had that distinctive yellow helmet – he had the kind of fire thing before I met him.

"1968 was tough. When Jimmy died, you started to worry. Before then I can't recall ever worrying too much about Mike having a big crash or thinking that he might die or end up injured in hospital. That changed in that awful, awful year."

Andrew Ferguson, the Lotus team manager, also hinted in his book *Team Lotus – The Indianapolis Years* that Mike was concentrating on other projects away from the sport without knowing the whole story. He was constantly approached by Mike to buy shares in an Australian timber company, but Mike was also talking of expanding the garage business in both America and Australia.

Mike said in an interview just before the start of the season: "I've had some fairly alarming crashes. I am sure my wife worries but she's very good, she has a lot of understanding. We badly want a family but not until I have stopped racing so much as otherwise we would never see each other. You become very narrow-minded if you're not careful, very involved in this world. You live out of a suitcase, in a rush, for the enormous satisfaction of doing a perfect lap or bringing to the finishing line a race car that is falling to bits."

In early April 1968, Mike gave an interview to the *Reading Evening Post* and some of his words became very quickly and sadly poignant: "Death is the last thing I ever think about when racing. Driving a car at up to 200mph requires tremendous concentration and you get very little time to think of anything other than the job in hand. If I ever thought of dying, I would not even get into a saloon car, let alone a single-seater racing car. Lynne is probably the only thing that interrupts my thoughts when I am racing. Being a driver is a hard life. One has to go from circuit to circuit with perhaps only a few hours a month at home. I am doing well if I have a total of two months of the year in England, a couple of days at a time. Usually, all I think about is either the car in front or the car behind, but now and then, especially if I am winning, I think of Lynne."

Mike qualified his comments about stepping into a normal car versus racing cars at astronomical speed: "There is a time and a place for everything and many think they are racing drivers. I cannot stand people who turn main roads into race tracks. I frequently drive up the A4 from Maidenhead to Reading and it frightens me to death. I would much sooner drive through Monza than drive through Hare Hatch. At least at Monza, every driver there is a professional and are aware of the ramifications of colliding with other people. On the A4, people who have not got racing cars and who are not on a race track drive flat out as though the chequered flag is waiting for them at Shepherd's House Hill. If racing drivers took half the chances this people do, the death toll would be fantastic."

So, in May 1968, Mike found himself at Indianapolis to start the qualification process for the Indianapolis 500. He was in a Lotus 56 gas turbine car, one of the quickest cars on the grid. But a little background is needed as to why this car was so feted and why Mike was chosen to drive it.

Andy Granatelli had been a fan of the turbine engine ever since 1952. Granatelli, along with his brothers, was a car entrant of many years' standing for the Indianapolis 500. A larger-than-life figure, his zeal and bombastic personality helped propel himself into a senior management role with STP, a lubricants provider. By 1968, he was one of the top car entrants around for Indianapolis. He ended up finally winning the event in 1969 with Mario Andretti driving a Hawk. He was at every Indianapolis 500 as a driver, entrant, sponsor or spectator from 1946 until 2012. He missed the 2013 event and died later that year aged 90.

Granatelli was impressed by the turbine's durability and fuel economy. Because it also needed no water and only two gallons of oil, with an engine that did not require maintenance, the crew could concentrate on the chassis more. Although a more expensive engine initially, Granatelli worked out that its life between overhauls was actually some 12 years.

Granatelli built his own turbine car, the STP Paxton Turbocar for 1967 and came very close to winning the race. Parnelli Jones, the driver, was ten miles away from winning when a bearing failed on the gearbox. USAC then decided to lower the turbine inlet annulus area for 1968, limiting the power, prompting Granatelli to sue USAC. Granatelli then did a deal with Lotus to build four-wheel-drive turbine Lotuses, the Lotus 56, but he was keen not to dominate the race too easily or they would be restricted even more.

When the Lotus 56 came out, all the signs looked promising. Arthur Birchall, a mechanic for Lotus, recalled to Andrew Ferguson for *Team Lotus – The Indianapolis Years*; "Granatelli had insisted to Jimmy Clark to sandbag his times. Andy had a court case with USAC at the time and he wanted us to play it very easy so as not to get anyone's backs up. All Jimmy said was 'It's fantastic'. Even run at reduced speed, Jimmy went at 161mph."

Although some people, including Sir Jackie Stewart, believed Mike was actually the second choice to replace Clark, Mike was actually chosen irrespective of the injury

that would befall the Scotsman soon after the announcement of Stewart to join Graham Hill in Indiana. Colin Chapman spoke to Andy Granatelli about adding Mike to the roster with Stewart and Hill, and Granatelli was immediately agreeable to the idea.

In his biography, *It was Fun!*, Tony Rudd, the BRM team manager, revealed more of the timeline. "We went back to Silverstone to find out why the handling of our car had deteriorated after the International Trophy race. At the same time, Lotus was there with Graham Hill testing the four-wheel-drive Indy turbine car. Just before lunch, Colin Chapman approached me and said, 'When you wrote to me after Jim Clark's death and said you would do anything to help, do you remember?' I said, slightly warily, 'Yes'. Colin replied 'Well, Graham has to go back to London and Pratt & Whitney need to go back to the United States in a few hours. Could Mike drive the car for a few laps to get some data for Pratt & Whitney?' I agreed.

"After we finished testing, Mike sidled up to me. I said 'I know, you want to drive it and Indianapolis.' He said, 'Yes, I will not let it interfere with Monte Carlo.' I had some difficulty in convincing Mr and Mrs Stanley that we should release him for Indianapolis, but no driver with red blood in his veins passes up a chance like that. I also hoped it would give him a little more confidence in himself."

That confidence factor was one of the main reasons behind the sanctioning of the agreement with Lotus but, to be honest, it pretty much all worked in BRM's favour. The schedule for Indianapolis did not clash with any Formula One events and his Indy tests would end with his departure directly to Spain for the Grand Prix on 8 May. As well as a confidence boost, if Mike did well at Indianapolis, it might lead to extra publicity and sponsorship for BRM. However, as Andrew Ferguson revealed in his book, if things had succeeded, then there could well be a Team Lotus Worldwide Racing agreement for Mike and he would be seconded to the STP Section of the programme. That would have led to a whole different discussion with Tony Rudd and Louis and Jean Stanley.

Colin Chapman, of course, knew all about Mike's ability to drive and develop. But Chapman had also noticed how shrewd and perceptive Mike's technical feedback was and, in 1967, the fact that he had used a semi-automatic Chaparral with great aplomb, meant Chapman felt Mike could adapt quickly to the 56's two-pedal set-up.

Jackie Stewart was ruled out of Indianapolis after he broke a scaphoid bone in his wrist after a crash in qualifying for a Spanish Formula Two championship race at Jarama. He takes up the narrative of his attempts to still compete: "I was not able to drive because the wrist had been broken at Jarama. Mike got the drive and I was there. I was still hoping to race though. I went to all the trouble of going to Indianapolis because there was a very famous basketball team in Indiana, one of the college university teams called the Indiana Hoosiers, and they all have hands like that [Author note: This was an interview on Zoom, so Sir Jackie shows me his outspread hand and points to his wrist] and I thought well they must've had problems with their wrists. So I went there and, of course, the guy gave me the exact same reading I got first of all in Spain, then in Switzerland, then in England. I went all over the world to try and get this thing fixed because it was going to take 20 weeks where I couldn't drive. As it turned out, I could drive a bit sooner as I got a cast made in Geneva here, but it was too late for the Indianapolis 500. But Mike took over that job well."

As Bob Dance told me, "Jackie Stewart may think he was supposed to replace Clark, but Spence was always first choice. Colin asked for him. He was up to the job, he was always the chosen chap."

So Mike was ensconced in the Lotus 56 of his own right and was raring to go. He very quickly impressed many people, both within Lotus and in the Speedway as a whole. Jim Pickles worked for some years as a mechanic for the Indianapolis 500 attempts made by Lotus and thus his time with Mike was quite short, especially so in 1968, as he was the mechanic for Graham Hill. However, he recalls that Mike certainly made a mark. "I only worked with Mike very briefly. I worked for some years on the Lotus Indycars and obviously 1968 was the only year he was there. He was definitely chosen for the drive once Jimmy died. He was *very* competitive. Both myself and Arthur Birchall were very impressed with him. It was his first time at the track, the first time at an oval, the first time in the car and the first time he had driven a four-wheel-drive turbine, but I cannot remember ever thinking that he did a slow lap."

Andrew Ferguson, in his book *Team Lotus at Indianapolis*: "Mike Spence was a really lovely fellow. He was quiet, unassuming, completely devoid of politics and without an axe to grind in any direction. He combined an increasingly fast style of driving with sensitivity and intelligence. He brought home the BRM's infamous H16-engined car many a time, a sure mark of his delicacy of touch."

Tanner Watkins, a motorsport writer in the US, published an article on the internet a few years ago. He searched through the archives to find that Mike took to the track very quickly indeed. "Not short on confidence, Spence remarked playfully that it was difficult for him to stay within the regulated speed limits for rookies testing at the Speedway due to his natural talent and perceived understanding of the car. When practice opened for the month and competitors began posting times, the Brit held tough in the top half of the

Mike was always good with the fans and especially picked up a new appreciative audience with the American fans at Indianapolis. *John Spence*

leader board. While quick, Spence negotiated the four corners noticeably lower than most drivers, slinging the car harder and narrower towards the apex than had typically been seen at the 2.5-mile oval. He received advice from multiple USAC officials and even the Chief Steward of IMS, Harlan Fengler, warning him that danger could be near should these driving patterns continue."

The first day of running saw Mike reach 155mph on average, with a 195mph top speed on the straights. Mike completed his rookie test on 3 May, finishing with the second fastest time of the day, 160.915mph. The same day, Indianapolis 500 veteran and former winner Parnelli Jones decided not to race the Granatelli-run STP turbine car. Jones felt it was too difficult to get anywhere near the front row and chose not to race.

On 5 May, Mike went at 165mph. It was clear he felt at ease with the track. Two days later, Mike did a quite brilliant lap at 169.555mph, just half a mph below Mario Andretti's then track record. Ten laps were done at 168mph and a further four over 169mph. Graham Hill did 169.045mph and Mike's time was even more remarkable as he had a full fuel load and there were strong winds. Mike and all at Team Lotus had finished for the day.

Colin Chapman then took part in an interview, where he talked about Jim Clark's death and how he wanted to quit and close Team Lotus, but contractual obligations and loyalty to his unwavering and dedicated staff brought him round. He seemed a bit more upbeat and Graham and Mike brought a large cake into the garage saying 'good luck'. On 7 May 1968, just hours before Mike's death, all seemed rosy for the Lotus camp.

The *Indianapolis Star* had printed its words for the day and Chapman was ebullient when he talked to them: 'Colin Chapman has to be one of the happiest men at the Speedway – in marked contrast to a year ago when the STP Lotus crew sweat blood and tears until the final day of qualification.

Chapman said, "It's always nice to come here and have things go right so quickly. The drivers have adapted so easily and swiftly to the track. We haven't had any major problems this year and that's wonderful. You always expect something. But we've been running hard and long because we have to leave today for the Spanish Grand Prix. We wanted to see if there were any major problems that would have to be handled in the week we're gone." The paper concluded, with Hill and Spence having finished their runs and as the fastest, that there had indeed been no major problems.

Jim Pickles: "The car itself was very easy to work on, very straightforward. Often with most cars, including the Lotus 38, which was an absolute nightmare to set up, you had to sort out the geometry of the car. In simple terms, there were three key elements that you needed to be consistent for optimum set-up. Most of the time, you'd fiddle around all day and all night to sort at least one of the issues out as the ride might be too high or too low and so on, but with the turbine it was pretty much perfect all the time. We had plenty of time and went out in the evenings! We found it a very easy car to get used to quickly and I suspect the drivers did too. Certainly Mike was very happy with the car. Although I worked with Graham [Hill], I don't remember Mike or Graham saying anything at all."

That should have been that. But then Greg Weld, STP's chosen driver in the third Lotus 56, had just passed his driver's refresher test but had been nowhere near the times posted by Team Lotus, and asked Andy Granatelli for help. Colin Chapman was asked by Granatelli if Mike could evaluate Weld's car but Chapman refused. Asked a second time later on, Chapman eventually relented.

Tanner Watkins: "It is the sportsmanlike gesture to drive another man's car in an attempt to help him find the meaning of Indy – speed. Such is the way of fate that Mike intended leaving Indianapolis that night for the Spanish GP with Graham Hill and then return for the Indy 500 race. However, towards the end of the day, with just 48 minutes left in practice, he was asked to test team-mate Greg Weld's turbine."

David Tremayne, a noted author, said in an article about Spence for *Grand Prix Plus* magazine that, 'Mike would have done anything, like Jim Clark, for the charismatic Lotus chief.' It is easy, when writing this to paint Weld as a hapless villain who shouldn't have been at the Speedway, but he was a very capable driver. Inducted in the National Sprint Car Hall of Fame in 1998, Weld finished in the top ten of his 36 USAC Championship Car series races eleven times, finishing fourth at Sacramento in 1970. He was also the 1967 USAC Sprint Car Series champion. However, Weld struggled to step up at Indianapolis. He was there seven times between 1965 and 1973, but only qualified the once, in 1970. Even then, he qualified on the back row of the grid. Otherwise, he had failed rookie tests or crashes in qualifying to his name. With Mike's advice and development knowhow, he could have definitely helped Greg with subtle technical advice to help the Kansas City native qualify.

Aside from those working either on the Spence or Weld cars, Bruce Boembeke was one of the last people to see Mike alive. A massive Indianapolis 500 enthusiast, he recalled his memories 50 years on to me: "It was early May and a very relaxed atmosphere. In those days, you could walk between the pit gate, and the garages [that space is famously called 'gasoline alley'] and often catch a driver in his street clothes and not surrounded by people wanting an autograph or interview. Sometimes they'd be in driving uniform, or their way to the car or back from a run.

"On this particular day, it was Mike Spence, walking alone, and when I called him out. He seemed pleasantly surprised to be recognised. I told him I followed F1, and we had a nice chat standing in the sun, about travelling, being away from home, the thrill of racing, and the significance of Indy to people of the US as compared to the Europeans and it being 'just another race' – except for the last place guy in the 500 getting more prize money than any winner of a grand prix! I don't recall the last thing we talked about, but it was cool. Then one of his crewmen came over and said, 'Hey Mike, car's ready, let's do some laps'. Mike looked back at me, we shook hands, he said 'thanks'. I wished him good luck and said I needed to get to work and there we parted."

"It took about 15 minutes to walk to my car parked in the infield, but you can hear the cars on track from about anywhere in the infield, especially if there is more than one on track. I felt good, a glow from the conversation with a real driver, the sun warm on my shoulders. I was driving out of the track on my way downtown to work listening to the radio that broadcast from the track, all day, live, when they announced that Mike Spence had just crashed. Then before I got to work the second announcement came that the news was not good, that Mike had been killed. I was numb. Was I one of the last to talk with him? How strange a feeling, to see his smile, to know I just shook hands with the man, and half an hour later he was dead.

"I only wish I knew or remembered more of that day, the conversation. He was so open, relaxed and willing to talk to a complete stranger! I think he was amazed that I knew who he was. His reaction to my calling out to him was one of those head-snapping 'what, who knows me?!' But I believe now that Mike was genuine. A regular guy who was just happy to be there as much as I was."

Mike and Colin chat about car set-up. Also in the picture is Derek Gardner (far left), later to become famous for designing the Tyrrell 001, 003 and P34 (among others), Bill Cowe (between Colin and Mike) and Dick Scammell (on the right by the car). To the far right, smoking his pipe, is Fred Cowley from Pratt & Whitney.
Indianapolis Motor Speedway

Dick Scammell MBE was one of the longest serving mechanics with Team Lotus and, by 1968, had morphed more into a management role with the team, working closely with Andrew Ferguson: "With Indy, we only had a small team. fve or six people for two to three cars. We normally went well at Indy. For the turbine, it was square one for us in some ways. It had not been run before, but of course, it went very well!"

Arthur Birchall, Lotus mechanic: "Mike tested the Lotus 56 at Silverstone. I think Jackie was to test the car but suffered from a wrist injury and could not drive it. We then went to Indy and Mike had to take his Rookie test. He found the test difficult to adjust to as the car wanted to go faster. Mike was warned by the USAC observers to keep within the test speed limits and not run too high out of the groove. After completion of his test, he was free to practice and put in some very fast laps, much against the USAC's official advice. On the day of his accident, he was still running hot and

high and the USAC marshal had the yellow lights on before he hit the wall."

Mike was lapping at 163mph when he hit the wall at turn one on his first lap out with Weld's car. It was observed that he had gone higher than normal on his entry into turn one. A lap later he was even higher still, and the chief observer had the yellow lights on before Spence had even made contact with the wall. The car slid 300 feet, hit the wall at 45 degrees, went along the concrete for about 400 yards, veered back down the track for 240 feet with the engine whining.

David Tremayne wrote for *Grand Prix Plus* magazine: "As soon as he realised he couldn't save the situation and that a shunt was inevitable, he let the car run along it. It would be a bit embarrassing, especially as he had a reputation as a guy who was kind to his machinery and very rarely damaged it, but the impact could be limited if he let the Lotus go where it wanted. But the right front wheel hurled back into the cockpit."

Dick Scammell: "Mike was doing a pretty good job. Then I remember him taking a whack against the wall. In those days, the wheels were threaded on so that, ironically, they did not bounce off and hurt anyway, so what happened to Mike was sheer bad luck. I went to hospital to see him and so did Andrew Ferguson. Colin Chapman came in and said 'I am going home, you and Andrew are in charge!' He just disappeared. He said, 'There's my briefcase, everything's in there you'll need. Don't try and contact me!' In his briefcase, it was revealed that Colin Chapman did not approve of Greg Weld driving and that he had wanted a thoroughly experienced Indycar driver instead. Well, in some senses, we did not know what to do, but then we just thought all we can do is do the best you can, and so that's what we did."

The impact into the wall removed the right-front wheel but it was restrained by a track rod, normally designed that they would not bounce across the track in case of a crash during the race. This track rod then meant the wheel catapulted into Mike's head. It tore off the white helmet he was using and left black tyre marks across it with the strap still fastened. Mike was inert in the car, with no other injuries. He was unconscious but critically ill.

The initial plan was to use Firestone's private jet to fly Mike to Washington and the best neurosurgeon in the country. Air traffic control gave the go ahead, but then the local hospital in Indianapolis confirmed Dr Paul Bucy, a Chicago surgeon, was at Indianapolis anyway and seeing to Mike. At 9pm local time, the hospital planned to conduct brain surgery to reduce the shock to Mike's system. But at 9.45pm, Mike was dead. Five days after his accident, his time was still unbeaten.

Bill Cowe, long-time Lotus mechanic who was there at Indianapolis: "I don't think Mike made any mistake. The problem was that he took a slightly different line into turn

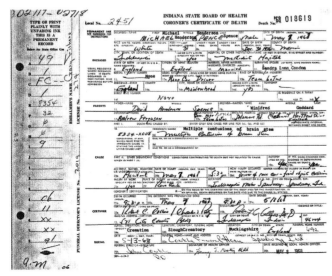

Mike's death certificate. *Richard Jenkins*

One. I think the car just got onto the marbles. As far as I can remember, the car was not damaged at all." Tony Rudd also confirmed in his biography that, "The other STP car had a different front-to-rear driver ratio, so it's angle of drift though the corners was slightly different to Mike's."

In response to safety fears over the turbine, Colin Chapman issued a frank rebuttal: "Both Andy Granatelli and I agreed that combination of four-wheel-drive and turbine power provides the safest kind of racing vehicles and this combination is here to stay. It should be obvious that the tragic accident which took Mike Spence had nothing to do with the design, power source or construction of the car, as has been further confirmed by the action today of Chief Steward Harlan Fengler in releasing these cars for further running."

Sir Jackie Stewart was initially quite hopeful about Mike's chances of survival, although he was perhaps not fully aware of the dire situation facing Mike. "When I saw him initially, he was clearly unconscious, but I was of the opinion that he would recover. Of course, we know now that the recovery never happened because the bang on the head was too much. He was the perfect team-mate for me to have at BRM and the sadness was he died in the car that I was supposed to drive. It is one of these examples that if there had been a halo there, he would still be with us."

Jackie Stewart mentioned the halo in April 2020 in our Zoom interview. The halo is a driver crash-protection system which consists of a curved bar placed to protect the driver's head. Since 2018, the FIA has made the halo mandatory on every vehicle in Formula One, Formula Two, Formula Three, Formula E and also Formula Four as a new safety measure. He said to me "Mike's death is one where you might want to make something of because a lot of people think that halos are unnecessary. When I was doing all the safety stuff, people thought that was unnecessary."

By December 2020, nobody in motorsport thought the halo was unnecessary. When Romain Grosjean, a French Formula One driver left the track at a 137mph on the opening lap of the Bahrain Grand Prix, he slammed into the Armco barriers at 53g with the car instantly erupting into fire. A crash of epic proportions, it was a throwback to an earlier and more dangerous time. The only reason Grosjean survived was because the halo pushed the barriers open, preventing a head injury at the point of impact. Despite the car being split in half and thoroughly frazzled, the halo remained intact during the whole drama. The halo had now convinced people. If it had existed before, it would have saved Mike and many other drivers including Ayrton Senna, Francois Cevert, Helmut Koinigg, Tom Pryce, Justin Wilson, Jules Bianchi, Maria de Villota and Henry Surtees, all of whom died when either being hit in the head by an object or crashing into Armco barriers with no protection against the impact.

Stewart carries on the narrative: "It was only appropriate for me to go and see him that evening after hearing that he had died. I went to the hospital that night and there was not a mark on his body. It was just that the wheel had come back and hit him on the helmet and with those speeds at Indianapolis, in turn one especially, the wheel rebounding back was awful fast, awful fast. It was a freak accident. It was a very sad day. It was a great loss, there's no doubt about that."

The local funeral home suggested a short memorial service should be held in the chapel that evening. They would post notices at the track for anyone who wished to attend. Andrew Ferguson revealed in *Team Lotus – The Indianapolis Years* that not a single empty seat was left. He wrote: "I was taken aback to see the senior level of those attending from other teams, without doubt due to them being so taken by Mike's sheer quality in the few days he had been at the Speedway."

The *Reading Evening Post* was one of many newspapers to quote Chapman immediately after Mike's death was confirmed: "I am filled with grief at the loss of my long-time friend and associate Jimmy Clark, and the additional loss just a month later to the day of Mike Spence. As an understandable result, I want nothing more to do with the 1968 Indianapolis race."

For the record, it is known that Mike Spence did not even attempt to qualify for an Indianapolis 500 – officially he is a non-qualifier with zero starts against his name. But, of course, he was never a zero. The *Indianapolis Star* summed up Mike's appeal and performance in a tribute later in May 1968: 'The Indianapolis Motor Speedway is not a place to which most drivers take easily. The two-and-a-half-mile oval of asphalt presents its own special problems to a driver. The high speeds make wind a big and varying factor around the race track. Each of the four corners looks the same but each is a little different. Some race drivers spend years trying to sort out the intricacies of the place without ever really mastering them.

"It is a seldom that a rookie comes along and then, straight out of the box, starts running faster than the veterans. That's not to say that there have not been precocious first-time drivers – Mario Andretti, Jim Hurtubise and Walt Faulkner all set lap records in their initial efforts here. Parnelli Jones and Jackie Stewart led major portions of their first race here. But it is doubtful if any man seemed to take to the Speedway quite as fast as Spence did.

"The 31-year-old Spence was a cut different from the fast Europeans we are used to seeing. His first day on the track saw him lap at 155mph which got him a reprimand from USAC as he had not actually taken his driver's test yet. Naturally, he whipped through that formality, effortlessly and

Mike in Australia enjoying a holiday at the start of 1968. Had all gone to plan, he could well have retired there at the end of the 1968 season.
Mike Spence/Lynne Spence

then once free to run at speeds of his own choosing Spence went fast. Almost immediately he climbed into the 165mph bracket and looked perfectly smooth in doing it.

"In addition, Mike was winning friends as quickly as he was lapping. He had a ready smile and a ready answer for any question. He laughed when kidded and kidded right back. In short, he was winning over the Speedway both on and off the track by the time 7 May rolled round."

Lynne Spence talked to me about Mike's death calmly and clearly. She was happy, some 52 years later to talk about it, maybe to exorcise something locked away all that time: "Mike's death was the only event I was never at. I went to all the race meetings, but of course, this was just testing. I was preparing, I think, for the Spanish Grand Prix. Mike had his bags packed to fly home and, of course, the stupid thing was it was not even his car. I got a telephone call from David Porter. I was in bed, or just about to go to bed, so it must've been around nine our time, or so, I think, when I got the telephone call. David said 'Mike's had a crash at Indy. Don't panic, they've taken him to the best hospital with the best brain surgeon in the country. Don't worry, he is in the best of hands.' So I thought, 'OK'."

"Then I spent the next couple of hours trying to find a phone number for his parents which proved very difficult. I cannot recall why but I think it was because they shared a phone number with another half-a-dozen farms in Australia. But I did finally get hold of his parents, spoke to both his mum and dad and said to them 'Do not worry he is in the best of hands'."

"I then told David to get me to Indianapolis as soon as possible on the first flight available and then... I swear this is gospel. I was lying in bed, feeling stressed and quite worried but not thinking the worst. I had a little round clock on the bedside table which was called a Baby Ben. It had a face like Big Ben and... this is absolutely gospel... whatever time it was that Mike died, that clock stopped and it never, ever, worked again. That's when I knew Mike had gone."

Epilogue

"He possessed the split-second reaction which is the hallmark of the expert. Mike was a skilful driver and a man of unassuming personality who possessed a genuine understanding of things mechanical"
Gregor Grant, journalist

Mike in the Lotus at the Nürburgring. *Nils Ruwisch archive*

ynne Spence: "Literally within seconds of the clock stopping, I heard screeching tyres. I was at Braebank apartments in Bray, right on the river, lovely, lovely place. David Porter was now at Bella Vista.

"Well, that was it. I do believe I shouted out a lot as I remember waking my neighbour, a lovely French lady who lived opposite us, and then a doctor arrived to give me sedatives. The next thing I remember is looking at Malcolm Angood at my bedside. There was also Mike's brother John and his wife Chris, and they stayed at Bella Vista for a bit. His mum and dad came a day two afterwards from Australia. I was gone and I couldn't do anything with the funeral. Credit where credit is due, David Porter sorted the funeral. I couldn't cope.

"It was at Bray Church just round the corner. I could have walked if I wanted to but I couldn't walk and the other two things I remember of that day is that, firstly, I have never seen, apart from when Princess Diana died, so many bunches of flowers in all my life, lined through the village, up towards the church, everywhere. The only other thing I remember was in the church itself. People started turning their heads around and so I looked and it was like I was seeing a ghost. It was Mike's brother John. They looked identical. It was scary, the resemblance, it was absolutely uncanny. I remember having a faint on the way out and Mike's mum and dad caught me. I remember thinking afterwards, 'What a silly cow, why did I do that?'"

Mike's funeral took place on 13 May 1968 at the picturesque St Michael's Parish Church in Bray, Berkshire. The church dates back to 1293 and needed to be sufficiently large as over 140 mourners piled in to pay tribute. Mike's brother John read the lesson as a veritable who's who of motor racing attended, which was testament indeed to Mike's standing.

Among the mourners were Colin Chapman (who Tony Rudd described as gaunt and grey), and his wife Hazel, Richard Attwood, Jack Brabham, Hugh Dibley, Graham Hill, David Hobbs, Innes Ireland and Stirling Moss. BRM was well represented by Sir Alfred Owen, Louis and Jean Stanley, Tim Parnell, Tony Rudd, Raymond Mays and Molly Wheeler, who represented the BRM Supporters Club. Representatives of the RAC, the British Racing Drivers' Club, the Goodwood Motor Circuit, Ford (Walter Hayes and Henry Taylor among them), the British Racing & Sports Car Club and even the Argentine Automobile Club attended, as well as Jimmy Stewart, Jackie's elder brother and a former grand prix driver himself. In addition, a number of wreaths were sent by a plethora of organisations ranging from firms Mike had direct links

BRAY PARISH CHURCH

MICHAEL HENDERSON SPENCE

Monday, 13th May, 1968
3 p.m.

The front of Mike's funeral notice sheet. *Ady Stimpson*

with (Lotus and Castrol, to name just two), but also from companies like Honda.

Upon his death, the employees at Mike Spence Ltd were also devastated. One unnamed worker told the *Reading Evening Post* on hearing the news: "When he was not racing, he would come here as much as he could. He was very much the sort of chap who you worked with rather than working for them." Peter Davies, the sales director of the firm at the time of Mike's death, added his comments to the paper: "Mike worked tremendously hard. He was all for the idea of the Maidenhead business and he backed it with all of his heart. The firm was started two years ago and Mike was chairman. He also provided a great deal of the financial backing. Mainly through his efforts we have become world famous in such a short time. He was one of the nicest people I know and great to work for. The whole of the racing world is going to be very sad at the loss of such a very dear friend."

Alan Rigarlsford: "It was a big shock when he died. I'll always remember where I was when I heard. I was having breakfast at the time, I lit the fire for the kids to come down, had my porridge and then I heard. I was absolutely gutted. I went to work but they sent everyone home and shut the company down for a couple of days. Then, very slowly and very quietly, we went back."

John Spence: 'It was a huge shock for all of us but all the moreso for my parents. Mike was at a stage where he could have lived anywhere in the world and the plan was for him to base himself with my parents in their Australian property, Nobby's Creek, near Muwillumbah in the far north of New South Wales. The scripture to 'Honour thy father and thy mother' came to me and as Christine, my wife, and I prayed about it. We agreed that we should now look at the possibility of moving out to them despite this meaning separation from Christine's family."

As a brief aside, John remains in Australia, as mentioned in the first chapter. David Spence died at the grand old age of 96 on 23 April 2006 in Southport, Queensland, Australia. Margaret Winifred Goddard, Mike's mother, was born on 12 November 1912 and died on the 1 October 2003 in Brisbane, Queensland, Australia. Both outlived their eldest son by over 35 years.

Lord Chesham (John Cavendish), executive vice chairman of the Royal Automobile Club paid this tribute to Mike on the day of his passing: "He had been fighting his way to the top for a number of years. It is doubly tragic that he should be killed when he seemed to be reaching his peak."

Former motorsport correspondent of *The Times*, John Blunsden recalled to Paul Fearnley in 2005: "Mike was maturing into a very accomplished driver. He was revealing a quality we perhaps had not realised he had. The real shame of it was that it was such an unnecessary accident, in that he was doing the decent thing, helping out another driver." Tim Parnell, in response to Blunsden's comment, said: "Well, that was typical of Mike. He was the nicest bloke I ever met in motor racing."

Mike's death caused very dark days at Team Lotus, in particular for Colin Chapman. There was even a possibility that Chapman would step away from the sport, this being one tragedy too far.

The below recollections are mainly either directly to me or Michael Oliver, in his 2009 book dedicated to the memories of the unsung heroes, *Tales from the Toolbox* or, in Tony Rudd's case, in his biography, *It was Fun!*

Hughie Absalom: "I was with Mike Spence when he was killed at Indianapolis. We were looking after his car and he went out and drove the Granatelli car, and that was what he got killed in. We were all right there when that happened, so

Mike relaxes on the river in Berkshire. *Lynne Spence*

that was not very nice. I can't imagine what it must be like for some of these guys that would have been working on the car that the guy got killed in. Fortunately, I never got into that. From there on you just build up this barrier. You just do the best you can and hope that everything is OK. You do know that you've got a guy's life in your hands but that's how it was. The real shame was working with the turbines was easy-peasy. I think if Spence had not been killed he would probably have won the whole Indianapolis 500 because he was flying."

Bob Dance: "Well, Indianapolis was dangerous. If anything went wrong, you were soon in trouble. Well, as you know, Jim came to grief and this was a huge stumbling block. It was really down, initially, to Graham Hill who in his typical English bulldog spirit 'pull yourself together lads' type style geed us up a little bit. We were still picking up the pieces when we heard Mike had come to grief.

"Now at that time I was at the Spanish border as I was heading to the Spanish Grand Prix. I used to hate going to Spain as they would mess us around for hours on end. I heard the news and went, 'Oh my goodness, the Old Man [Chapman] will stop racing now.' We carried on and that's when Graham came into his own. We had the brand new car for Graham; we only had one car entered anyway for that race. Graham did well with the new car and that cheered us up. He took us all out to dinner with his wife Bette and, again, gave us a real boost.

"I am sure the guv'nor, had he been there, would not have wanted the new car for Graham. But all went well, Graham won and it geed us up again. I am sure that was why Colin came back because we were winning and he enjoyed the highs as much as he hated the lows."

Tony Rudd: "I always felt that Colin took Jim Clark's death extremely well, as if he had mentally conditioned himself to the fact it may happen one day. But the death of Mike, so soon afterwards, really seemed to hurt him. He gradually hardened and there was further significant change later on when Jochen Rindt died in 1970 and then finally, when Ronnie Peterson died in 1978."

Jackie Stewart (left, back to camera) talks to Mike at the 1967 South African GP. Team manager Tony Rudd is on the far right.

Dunlop South Africa Ltd Technical Department/John Spence

Bob Sparshott: "We came very close to finishing at Team Lotus when Mike died. It was almost the straw that broke the camel's back. If it had not been for Graham Hill, I think it would have ended. We were very, very, very close to finishing. We went to Spain not really sure if we would carry on. I think the thing was, ironically our cars were safer in 1968. I mean earlier in the decade, they were lethal. They had aluminium, they had fuel tanks, they were constructed a particular way. If you had a crash you were in big trouble. And then with a safer set of cars, we had two guys die – Jimmy and Mike."

Sparshott revealed a little more just prior to my contact with him to Ivan Ostroff of *Classic Cars* magazine about just how it had affected Chapman: "When Jimmy Clark was killed, we weren't sure if the team would carry on as Colin just disappeared. Then we heard Mike Spence had been killed at Indianapolis so we were sure that would put a lid on it, but still heard nothing, so we carried on. We won [the Spanish Grand Prix] and it was a real morale boost, yet we'd still heard nothing from Chapman. We'd brought the prototype Lotus 49B with the wedge tail with us but were told not to run it because the old man had not seen it.

"At Monaco, we had it under wraps but there was still no sign of Chapman. After first practice, we went back to our hired garage. In the evening, Chapman came breezing in, told Bob Dance to take the cover off the 49B and then dictated two pages of things to alter overnight so the car could run the next day. It was 9pm and I blew a gasket. But Chapman put his arm around me like a father and said, 'Now what's the matter, Bob'? I said, 'It's ridiculous. We've been carrying this car around for two race meeting and you suddenly want us to

run it. We're not ready.' But Chapman could talk the birds off the trees and gave me a pep talk about staying ahead of the opposition. So we worked all night and, of course, we won. The Old Man was back as if nothing had ever happened."

However Jim Pickles, who was based at Indianapolis when the crash happened, had a different take on the immediate future of Lotus, as he recalled to me: "When Jimmy died, Colin went off for a short while and he was in the pit of despair, understandably. Andrew Ferguson and Dick Scammell called us all together for a meeting and we resolved that whatever happened with Colin, we would continue to keep Lotus going for as long as we could; Andrew would lead the team if Colin never came back. Then when Mike died, at that time the Old Man was... it hit him hard, and he virtually pulled out. Andrew reconfirmed that we'd carry on at Indianapolis, we would carry on at Spain and just keep going. Andrew Ferguson virtually held us together and said 'Come on, we've got to do something.' And we did. It was difficult to deal with, but there's a little bit of 'got to get on with it'. It affects different people differently of course. We were in better shape then. I was certainly a bit more experienced, the cars were better, we were having proper sleep because the cars were behaving properly and, of course, that doesn't half make a difference."

Bill Cowe: "When Mike was killed, well, after that, I did not get too close to drivers any more. Mike was such a genuine, lovely, nice man. Very easy-going. He was always grateful of anything you did and was not demanding in any way. I was very fond of him. When he died, I kind of did what the others did and concentrated on the car itself and did not really focus on the driver on a personal level. It's all you could do, just do the job to the best of your abilities, and our job was to get the car working the best it could. It's got to be remembered how quick he was at Indy. He was only a rookie, but he was *very* quick and he was getting quicker. He would have been in the running to win I think.

"Mike really developed much more at BRM. In fact, ever since he left Lotus as he developed at Parnell and then he was mightily quick at BRM and was showing a lot more promise. Maybe it was just he was in a different environment, maybe he worked better with Tim, maybe it was because he was not with Jimmy but he was at his peak when he came to Indianapolis."

Arthur Birchall: "I went back out to Indianapolis in May and Mike Spence was killed on 7 May. That came as a hell of a shock. Well, the way we dealt with that was that Jim Endruweit went out and bought four black ties, we went to a memorial service for him at the funeral parlour in Indiana and then got on with our work the following day, that's the way it went."

Obviously it was not just Lotus that was left bereft. Everyone at BRM would have felt particularly distraught that someone who was at their peak of their powers had died

Mike Spence, 1967. *John Spence*

in an event that they had no involvement with. So much so, that in his book, *It was Fun!*, Tony Rudd revealed that Pedro Rodriguez came up to him, realising how close everyone was to Mike, suggesting that if the team wished to withdraw from the Spanish Grand Prix as a mark of respect, he would fully understand. In response to the Mexican's magnanimous gesture, Rudd said: "I felt and I told Pedro this, we can't sit around and mope, we have to go out and win. That's the best mark of respect we can show Mike."

Lesley Appel, Tony Rudd's daughter, reveals that it was not just Colin Chapman who was deeply affected by Mike's death. "Mike was absolutely lovely, I have always believed his death was a big factor in dad leaving Formula One. Just a couple of weeks before we had been at Bacton, Norfolk, which was for the Easter holidays, I guess. Mike came and joined us and we went sailing. I can still remember the day now. It was absolutely freezing and we had none of the wet cold weather gear we have now. I know we were at Acle Bridge and we, as was the norm in those days, went to the pub afterwards. My sister and I were left in the porch while Mike and dad went inside.

"I am sure this would count as child abuse now, but we did not mind a bit; we got a coke with a straw and crisps, they got beer and a roaring fire! Mike was one of the nice ones, so warm and friendly and we thought he was wonderful. I was all of eight or nine years old and still remember, we could sail a bit, but he was much more patient with us than dad was."

Tony Rudd also refers to the sailing trip in his book, *It Was Fun!* Funnily enough, he doesn't mention leaving his children out in the freezing cold with crisps and coke, but he did reveal a bit more about Mike's wishes. "He confessed to me that he had a yearning to drive at Indianapolis. I gave him another pep talk along the lines of, 'You are much too much a gentleman on the track. This is a hard business. Get in there and do some pushing and shoving.' We also hatched the idea that weekend of the Spence Elan programme, basically using a BRM Green Lotus Elan with Spence suspension improvements and a BRM-built two-phase Lotus Twin-Cam."

Back to Lesley Appel: "Colin was far more human than people seem to think. My understanding is he always sort of accepted that Jimmy might die, but Mike really pushed him to the edge. Whereas, with my dad and his own reaction to Mike's death, I feel he blamed himself for letting Mike take the drive. I know that after Mike's death, dad started talking to Rolls-Royce about going back to them and those talks went on and on.

"I remember Jochen Rindt dying was truly awful for Colin. In so many ways it was a truly awful time. Jackie Stewart was brave to take a stand; the deaths would never be accepted now. I remember talking to Bette Hill many years later and asking how she lived with the fear. She told me that she quite literally blanked it out, Graham would not have stopped anyway."

Tony Rudd confirmed as much in his biography: "Pam [Rudd, Tony's wife] sensed Mike's death had gone deep, not helped by such remarks as 'His death will forever be on your conscience'. I found it much harder to connect with the team, even moreso than after recent BRM disasters and the departure of Graham Hill and Jackie Stewart. Mike and I had talked for an hour about Indy. He had some bad thoughts about getting back in a Lotus but he knew it was a great opportunity. The day he died was one of my darkest days in some 15,000 working days. Mike was on the threshold of what promised to be his best ever season.

"He would paint this wonderful word picture of what a car was doing and, because he was a decent bloke, he would always preface his remarks with the words, 'If it were my money on it, I would...' whenever suggesting a modification. Losing him was such a huge blow for us," he later told David Tremayne who recalled the conversation for *Grand Prix Plus* magazine.

Richard Attwood was chosen to replace Mike at Monaco a few weeks later (although it should have been Chris Irwin, but he was never to race again after suffering terrible head injuries less than two weeks after Mike's death), and he remembers both the situation and the initial reaction: "I spent quite some time with Mike and Lynne in South Africa during the 1967 Springbok series where we were a group all travelling to the same places. They were together most of the time but we had meals and sessions together and fitted in well. After Mike died, I spent some time with Lynne who was distraught and being supported by the racing crowd, mostly around Maidenhead area.

"Mike did not seem to have any side to him and fitted in perfectly among all of us. As racing guys together, generally it takes someone with an attitude problem not to get on with like-minded folk, and he was not the odd one out. He seemed a really nice guy without any foibles. So I got the call to replace him for the Monaco Grand Prix. The call was very late and I arrived in Monte Carlo when there was also a strike on in France.

"Louis Stanley, director at the BRM team, saw me at Nice airport and asked me what I was doing there! Can you imagine that?! Even he did not know I was going to race for BRM! Once he learnt why I was there, he was incensed that I was driving 'his' car because he thought I was not good enough, so much so that he wants the car to be entered by Tim Parnell's private team to hide the disgrace that is about to happen. So my race number became 15 and not the lower number of 5 which I think was the works number.

Ready for action. *John Spence*

"If there was any upset about Mike, I did not see it. As it was, I was arriving there in a great rush, and trying to seize a great opportunity that may happen only once in a lifetime. Unfortunately, these sort of things [drivers dying] happened frequently and there was no time by anyone involved to dwell on such matters."

Attwood, always a Monaco specialist, finished second, which was anything but a disgrace. Len Terry, the famed designer who worked for Lotus and BRM among others, was of the opinion, which he gave to Paul Fearnley in an article in *Motor Sport* in 2005, that: "Richard did a great job, but I genuinely think Mike Spence could have won that day if it had been him in the car."

For BRM, they felt the loss of a superb development driver keenly. As David Tremayne recalled in his articles on Mike for both *Motor Sport* and *Grand Prix Plus*: "The season held great promise, as Peter Wright, then a fledgling design engineer, confirmed. 'Mike was just a lovely guy, and I really believe that BRM's demise began with his death. He was obviously going places. Mike was in tune with the team and Tony, and he was exactly what BRM needed. He was pretty obviously on the rise. He was a very good test driver, he was in tune with the car and he could communicate. You know how it is when you get together with a driver and suddenly start to make progress.

"Mike was the team's big hope, and he was making it all start to click. BRM's ability to develop its car died with Spence. Rodriguez showed great form until mid-season, but then the early promise simply evaporated."

Tony Rudd also confirmed as such in Adam Cooper's biography of Piers Courage, *Last of the Gentlemen Racers*: "While we were still free-wheeling with Mike Spence's setting up ability, we would have an edge. After we lost all that Mike had contributed, which took two or three races to run out,

Chapter 13

Richard Attwood didn't contribute very much. In fact, he went to a lot of trouble to keep out of it! Pedro didn't have a clue! So it all went downhill."

The tributes to Mike either at the time, in previous interviews and in discussions with this book are overwhelmingly positive, as you will see below.

Tim Parnell: "Mike was a brilliant test driver. Chapman valued him highly in that respect. That's why he asked him over. He was a capable, thoughtful, unassuming, a model professional."

David Piper: "I knew Mike Spence quite well. He was definitely one of the best."

Sir Jackie Stewart: "Mike was smooth and unspectacular, a solid performer who had a good relationship with the engineers. But he never pushed himself forward for a drive and always seemed destined to be a very good number two. Mike was almost too nice to be a racing driver. He was very well mannered and very shy, almost introverted. The kind of person you would have expected to have had Jim Clark as a team-mate which, of course, he did.

"Mike was a very clean driver and he was one of those that you could race against. Some of them were a little enthusiastic, to say the least! Mike was a perfect gentleman off the track as much as he was on the track. We did not spend a lot of time together but I did think it was a good choice for him to be driving the Indycar because that would have been my third Indy race and, when I couldn't do it, he was the right man to get the seat there's no doubt about that. He drove the Elans as well. He and Peter Arundell.

"He was a quiet man, no show about him, he was not extravagant in any way. A very good driver. I was doing my best to keep up with him at the 1965 Race of Champions at Brands Hatch and I couldn't. He was in a very good car, a fast car, no doubt, but he still drove it well. He did not put the car under such stress as others."

It appeared Spence and Stewart got on well and there is one telling incident that the *Winnipeg Free Press* reported in August 1967. Most of motor racing is familiar with Sir Jackie as the model professional, but it appears Mike, as much as he enjoyed the sport, was even more professional

Mike at the Race of Champions, 1967. **Ted Walker**

as the paper recalled a recent evening's conversation at the French Grand Prix. "The next night, Jackie Stewart stopped by Dan Gurney's table, possibly hoping to get information about gear ratios. Gurney stretched out with a plate of cheese and grinned mischievously and persuaded Jackie to sit with him and have a glass of wine. Mike Spence, standing at the stairs called out 'Come to bed Jackie, don't josh about'. The Scotsman duly nodded and bade Gurney his farewell. Gurney smiled and headed over to the television and tried to find a cowboy western movie to watch."

Gregor Grant in his tribute to Mike in *Speedworld International* magazine just after Mike's passing was fulsome in his praise for Spence: "He possessed the split-second reaction which is the hallmark of the expert. A natural test driver, he was of immense value to BRM. I always had great admiration for Mike and he right well backed up the little Scotsman Jim Clark. They got on well and Mike always said that he learned more from Clark than anyone else. With the H16, he tried harder than anyone else to make it work. This year he had emerged as a real tiger. Sadly, it was not to be. Motor racing is all the poorer for the loss of a grand sportsman, a skilful driver and a man of unassuming personality who possessed a genuine understanding of things mechanical."

Peter Davies: "I never felt Mike got the proper car for most of his career. He was at a good team, but it was the second-in-line car. Every time Mike had a proper car, a car he could do well in, he did so. He showcased his talent. He won the BOAC race, he won the South African Grand Prix, did brilliantly at the Race of Champions in 1968, was great in the Chaparral. When everything was first-in-line for him, he nailed it. Of course, that was the same with Indianapolis. He took straight to it."

Alan Henry, veteran journalist and author: "Mike had a gregarious charm, a grin that lit up the whole of his face. He was a serious professional, totally committed to his career but never ceased to gain the same sort of pleasure from racing in 1968 to his days in Formula Junior and before."

Autosport magazine's obituary, written by a very young Simon Taylor: "Mike Spence was one of the finest all-rounders in motor racing. His career was epitomised by driving that was very fast, smooth and intelligent. His ability to preserve a car and bring it to the finish made him much sought-after."

Jerry Entin, a very successful sports car driver in the United States: "I feel had he not tested someone else's car at Indy, Mike Spence would have been a world beater. He was respected by every single Formula One driver. As far as I am concerned, he appeared to be a second coming. Mike Spence was as good a driver as I had ever seen. He was nothing short of unbelievable in that McLaren Mk2."

David Hobbs: "He was a very talented driver, I think he was too nice. Well, he got mad at me for winning that race at Roskilde but he was not cut in the same mould as the likes of Ayrton Senna or Michael Schumacher, he did not have that ruthless streak. Jim Clark and Jackie Stewart had that too, but in a different way.

"He went a bit further than I did, but then his luck ran out. But yeah, he was a very talented, competent driver and I think he could have done well in Formula One. He was good enough to be up there in the championship running all the time. Not quite good enough to be champion though. He used to score points in most races, but in those days, the cars were so unreliable, every race was not a case of am I going to win it, but am I going to finish it?

"He was a good competent driver, maybe lacking a bit of push and drive, just not ambitious enough. In those days, the ambition was to stay alive and anything else was a bonus from there on. We were good but we were never going to be as good as Jimmy Clark or Mario Andretti or Lewis Hamilton.

So Mike was now gone, but Lynne remained. However, she revealed that being a racing widow was a lonely existence. "You had a lot of people around you at the time and then, two weeks later, you were on your own. Mike's mum and dad stayed around for about two to three weeks. John and Chris went back to their children. I did not know myself if I would go back to South Africa. Sally Swart [Jim Clark's long-time girlfriend] would have helped but she was in turmoil over Jim. Bette Hill did not help with the 'Doghouse Club'. [Author note: The Doghouse Club or, to give it the official title of the Women's Motor Racing Associates Club, was a support network for women involved in motorsport, which included both women drivers and wives and partners of racing drivers.] Ginnie Parnell, Loti Irwin and Norma Robb [Frank Williams' secretary] a helped a bit.

"I was angry then but I am not now. I reminded them of death and they wanted to move on with their lives. But also... what do you say to people? To be fair, a lot of the racing wives, I only knew well enough to say hello and that was it. There were very few that really were close.

"I had a good friend called Norma Robb who I asked, after a while, to share the flat in Bray. She was secretary to Frank Williams who at that time had just started his racing team. Well, Frank was so broke, he would sleep on our couch in Bray and I would buy him takeaways or cook him food. Norma was such good friend to me, it was one way to repay her."

Before too long, Lynne moved back to South Africa. She met a Welshman, David Martin, who was a pilot for

Mike at Silverstone for the BRDC International Trophy, 29 April 1967.
Autocar/John Spence

South Africa Airways and married him in the early 1970s. They now live in a nice home in Wales and have two children and two grandchildren. There is a memorial to Mike still, where his ashes were interred, which can be found in Slough Cemetery and Crematorium, in Berkshire, England. It is in plot D152 and remains well cared for.

It is over 50 years since Mike died, but he is far from forgotten. Although this is partly due to a generation that either raced against him or grew up watching him race, it is likely that Mike will still be remembered, irrespective of anything this book will do to help, because he was an integral part of a truly iconic era in history. In addition, Classic Team Lotus does such a fantastic job with its legacy that most of their key drivers, of which Mike was one, are feted long after their career ended via historic festivals and other similar events.

I will give the last word to Mike's good friend, the late Malcolm Angood: "I worked with Lotus and Jimmy Clark, but when Lotus moved to Norwich, I stopped. I'd just got married. I worked in the sales and service department at Mike Spence Ltd. I stayed there until May 1968. I left at the end of the same week Mike was killed. If he was not there, I was not going to stay there.

Mike was an A1, 100 percent, fantastic guy. Very loyal to Lotus, always loyal to the team – or whatever team, really. He should have been more forceful and, as a quiet man, he did not push himself forward more. But what he did was show people how good he was with his race results. And when people like Colin Chapman and Jim Hall choose you, you're doing something right. Jim Hall, in particular, could have chosen so many people to go with Phil Hill, but he specifically chose Mike. That says a lot."

Appendix: Race Results

Date	Race	Circuit	No	Car	Entered by	Qualified	Race Result	Notes
1/1/1957	Rallying			Turner 950	M H Spence	Unknown		
1/1/1958	Goodwood 5 lap handicap	Goodwood		AC Bristol	M H Spence	Unknown	4th	
1/1/1958	race	Silverstone		AC Bristol	M H Spence	Unknown	2nd	
1/1/1958	race	Silverstone	98	AC Bristol	M H Spence	Unknown	Unknown	
1/1/1959	Raced in AC					Unknown		
6/6/1959	BARC Goodwood 34th Members Meeting sportscar race	Goodwood	103	AC Bristol	M H Spence	Unknown	4th	
27/6/1959	BARC Goodwood 35th Members Meeting sportscar race	Goodwood	63	Turner	M H Spence	Unknown	4th	
27/6/1959	BARC Goodwood 1150 sportscar race	Goodwood	63	Turner	M H Spence	n/a	DNA	Drove AC in Handicap race instead
19/3/1960	FJ Race BARC Members	Goodwood	28	Cooper 52	M H Spence	6th	6th	
27/3/1960	FJ Race Snetterton MRC	Snetterton	43	Cooper 52	Coburn Engineers	4th	5th	
2/4/1960	FJ Race BARC Spring National	Oulton Park	24	Cooper 52	Coburn Engineers	8th	6th	
18/4/1960	Chichester CUP BARC Easter Monday	Goodwood	66	Cooper 52	Coburn Engineers	7th	6th	
18/4/1960	Lavant Cup Formula 2 Race	Goodwood	38	Cooper 45	Peter Westbury	16th	14th	
24/4/1960	Fj Race BRSCC Meeting	Snetterton	23	Cooper 52	Coburn Engineers	2nd	2nd	
14/5/1960	FJ Race Silverstone International Trophy Meeting	Silverstone	2	Cooper 52	Coburn Engineers	9th	5th	
22/5/1960	FJ Race Snetterton MRC	Snetterton	36	Cooper 52	Coburn Engineers	1st	1st	Also took fastest lap
6/6/1960	Cheshire Cup	Oulton Park	14	Cooper 52	Coburn Engineers	2nd	2nd	joint fastest lap
19/6/1960	Eastern Counties 100 mile	Snetterton	19	Cooper 52	Coburn Engineers	5th	8th	
29/6/1960	Gran Premio della Lotteria Heat 1	Monza	11	Cooper 52	D B Porter	3rd	1st	Won after 15 laps, 86.215km, 169.672kph
29/6/1960	Gran Premio della Lotteria Final	Monza	11	Cooper 52	D B Porter	2nd	DNF	Retired after engine failure lap 22 of 30
3/7/1960	Grand Prix de la Chatre FJ race	La Châtre		Cooper 52	Coburn Engineers	Unknown	7th	Inititally retired after 28 laps with an accident but rejoined and was still running, unclassified, in seventh place. Achieved fastest lap
16/7/1960	FJ Race British GP Meeting	Silverstone	25	Cooper 52	Coburn Engineers	7th	5th	
1/8/1960	John Davy Trophy	Brands Hatch	63	Cooper 52	Coburn Engineers	9th	9th	
20/8/1960	BARC FJ Championship Heat 2	Goodwood	4	Cooper 52	Coburn Engineers	6th	5th	
20/8/1960	BARC FJ Championship Final	Goodwood	4	Cooper 52	Coburn Engineers	14th	9th	
24/9/1960	FJ Race North Staffs MC	Silverstone	122	Cooper 52	Coburn Engineers	Unknown	1st	Fastest Lap
24/9/1960	F.Libre Race N Staffs MC	Silverstone	122	Cooper 52	Coburn Engineers	Unknown	2nd	
9/10/1960	Fj Race BRSCC Meeting	Snetterton	49	Cooper 52	Coburn Engineers	6th	DNF	Retired on the 1st lap after an accident
16/10/1960	Lewis-Evans Trophy Formula 2	Brands Hatch	37	Cooper 45	Peter Westbury	9th	DNF	Retired after 13 laps
15/4/1961	FJ Race BARC Spring National	Oulton Park	71	Emeryson	Emeryson Cars	n/a	DNA	Car not ready
22/4/1961	FJ Race Aintree 200 Meeting	Aintree	71	Emeryson	Emeryson Cars	n/a	DNA	Car not ready
6/5/1961	FJ Race Silverstone International Trophy Meeting	Silverstone	34	Emeryson	Emeryson Cars	n/a	DNS	Reserve entry
22/5/1961	Anerley Trophy	Crystal Palace	52	Emeryson	Emeryson Cars	n/a	DNA	At Goodwood
22/5/1961	FJ Race Whit Monday National	Goodwood	79	Emeryson	Emeryson Cars	8th	DNF	Retired after 3 laps due to overheating engine
3/6/1961	John Davy Trophy	Brands Hatch	82	Emeryson	Emeryson Cars	28th	DNF	Did not practice; retired lap 1 clutch (new car)
18/6/1961	Eastern Counties 100 mile	Snetterton	44	Emeryson	Emeryson Cars	Unknown	12th	
8/7/1961	FJ Race 2 British Empire Trophy Meeting	Silverstone	42	Emeryson	Emeryson Cars	7th	9th	
23/7/1961	Solitude F1 Grand Prix	Solitude	8	Emeryson-Climax	Emeryson Cars	11th	DNF	Broken gearbox on lap 6
23/7/1961	John Law Trophy	Snetterton	93	Emeryson	Emeryson Cars	n/a	dna	
29/7/1961	Commander Yorke Trophy 100 mile Race	Silverstone	31	Emeryson	Emeryson Cars	Unknown	1st	Fastest Lap. Won after 63 laps, 201.84 kms
7/8/1961	John Davy Trophy	Brands Hatch	76	Emeryson	Alan Brown	21st	DNF	Retired after a crash lap 14 of 20
12/8/1961	Silverstone 6 Hours Relay Handicap	Silverstone		AC Bristol			6th	
19/8/1961	BARC FJ Championship Heat 1	Goodwood	31	Emeryson	Emeryson Cars	5th	6th	
19/8/1961	BARC FJ Championship Final	Goodwood	31	Emeryson	Emeryson Cars	11th	6th	
2/9/1961	September Trophy Heat 1	Crystal Palace	9	Emeryson	Emeryson Cars	9th	6th	
2/9/1961	September Trophy Final	Crystal Palace	9	Emeryson	Emeryson Cars	10th	9th	
1/10/1961	Lewis-Evans Memorial Trophy F1 race	Brands Hatch	15	Emeryson-Climax	Emeryson Cars	2nd	2nd	
7/10/1961	FJ Race BRDC Clubman's Championship	Silverstone	63	Emeryson	M H Spence	Unknown	9th	
7/10/1961	F.Libre Race BRDC Clubman's Championship	Silverstone	63	Emeryson	M H Spence	Unknown	6th	
14/4/1962	FJ Race Lombank International Meeting	Snetterton	53	Lotus 22	Ian Walker Racing	2nd	6th	
23/4/1962	Chichester CUP BARC Easter Monday	Goodwood	41	Lotus 22	Ian Walker Racing	4th	3rd	
28/4/1962	FJ Race Aintree 200 Meeting	Aintree	54	Lotus 22	Ian Walker Racing	12th	4th	
12/5/1962	FJ Race Silverstone International Trophy Meeting	Silverstone	24	Lotus 22	Ian Walker Racing	6th	6th	
2/6/1962	GP de Monaco Junior Heat 1	Monte Carlo	126	Lotus 22	Ian Walker Racing	2nd	3rd	
2/6/1962	GP de Monaco Junior Final	Monte Carlo	126	Lotus 22	Ian Walker Racing	4th	2nd	
11/6/1962	Anerley Trophy Heat 1	Crystal Palace	62	Lotus 22	Ian Walker Racing	1st	2nd	
11/6/1962	Anerley Trophy Final	Crystal Palace	62	Lotus 22	Ian Walker Racing	2nd	2nd	
11/6/1962	BARC National Open Sportscar race	Crystal Palace	32	Lotus 23	Ian Walker Racing	n/a	DNA	Raced in F2 race instead
24/6/1962	Gran Premio della Lotteria Final	Monza	21	Lotus 22	Ian Walker Racing	2nd	DNF	Retired after a crash on lap 9 of 30
24/6/1962	Gran Premio della Lotteria Heat 2	Monza	21	Lotus 22	Ian Walker Racing	1st	2nd	
1/7/1962	FJ Race Final	Reims	50	Lotus 22	Ian Walker Racing	12th	1st	Won after 10 laps, 83 kms
1/7/1962	FJ Race Heat 2	Reims	50	Lotus 22	Ian Walker Racing	3rd	7th	
8/7/1962	FJ Race Part 1 GP de l'ACF Mtg	Rouen	38	Lotus 22	Ian Walker Racing	4th	DNF	Retired after 18 laps with gearbox failure
8/7/1962	FJ Race Part 2 GP de l'ACF Mtg	Rouen	38	Lotus 22	Ian Walker Racing	23rd	3rd	

Mike at the British Grand Prix, 1967. *Harold Barker/John Spence*

Date	Race	Circuit	No	Car	Entered by	Qualified	Race Result	Notes
8/7/1962	FJ Race Aggregate GP de l'ACF Mtg	Rouen	38	Lotus 22	Ian Walker Racing	3rd	8th	Retired after 38 laps with gearbox failure
15/7/1962	Trophee D'Auvergne	La Charade, Clermont-Ferrand	47	Lotus 23	Ian Walker Racing	n/a	DNA	In entry list with Peter Ryan but Ryan was killed two weeks previously
15/7/1962	FJ Race Part 1	Charade	64	Lotus 22	Ian Walker Racing	4th	4th	
15/7/1962	FJ Race Part 2	Charade	64	Lotus 22	Ian Walker Racing	4th	7th	
15/7/1962	FJ Race Aggregate	Charade	64	Lotus 22	Ian Walker Racing	n/a	5th	
6/8/1962	BRSCC International Guards Trophy for Sportscars	Brands Hatch	24	Lotus 23	Ian Walker Racing	10th	9th	2nd in class
6/8/1962	John Davy Trophy	Brands Hatch	39	Lotus 22	Ian Walker Racing	2nd	3rd	
18/8/1962	BARC FJ Championship	Goodwood	25	Lotus 22	Ian Walker Racing	2nd	DNF	Retired after 17 laps with gear linkage problems
25/8/1962	Copenhagen Cup	Roskilde	15	Lotus 22	Ian Walker Racing	n/a	DNA	car driven by Paul Hawkins
1/9/1962	London Trophy	Crystal Palace	21	Lotus 22	Ian Walker Racing	2nd	2nd	joint fastest lap
9/9/1962	GP du Midi-Pyrénées Languedoc Heat 2	Albi	11	Lotus 22	Ian Walker Racing	2nd	2nd	
9/9/1962	GP du Midi-Pyrénées Languedoc Final	Albi	11	Lotus 22	Ian Walker Racing	2nd	2nd	
29/9/1962	Vanwall Trophy	Snetterton	95	Lotus 22	Ian Walker Racing	17th	2nd	4th in L'Equipe FJ Rankings
29/9/1962	FJ Race North Staffs MC	Silverstone	141	ETA	D Lockspeiser	n/a	dna	Racing at Snetterton
21/10/1962	1000km Paris sportscar race	Linas-Monthlery, Paris	43	Lotus 23	Ian Walker Racing	n/a	DNA	On Entry list with Peter Arundell
6/4/1963	FJ Race BARC Spring National	Oulton Park	85	Lotus 27	Ron Harris – Team Lotus	n/a	DNA	Car not ready
15/4/1963	Chichester CUP BARC Easter Monday	Goodwood	108	Lotus 27	Ron Harris – Team Lotus	21st	8th	Did not practice
27/4/1963	FJ Race Aintree 200 Meeting	Aintree	32	Lotus 27	Ron Harris – Team Lotus	4th	5th	
11/5/1963	FJ Race Silverstone International Trophy Meeting	Silverstone	23	Lotus 27	Ron Harris – Team Lotus	12th	9th	
11/5/1963	Silverstone International GT sportscar race	Silverstone	26	Lotus Elan	The Chequered Flag	n/a	DNA	
25/5/1963	GP de Monaco Junior Heat 1	Monte Carlo	56	Lotus 27	Ron Harris – Team Lotus	2nd	DNF	Retired after a crash lap 10 of 16
3/6/1963	Anerley Trophy Heat 1	Crystal Palace	22	Lotus 27	Ron Harris – Team Lotus	6th	DNF	Retired after 3 laps with suspension failure
23/6/1963	GP de Rouen Heat 2	Rouen	4	Lotus 27	Ron Harris – Team Lotus	2nd	3rd	
23/6/1963	GP de Rouen Final	Rouen	4	Lotus 27	Ron Harris – Team Lotus	5th	4th	
30/6/1963	FJ Race GP de l'ACF Meeting	Reims	4	Lotus 27	Ron Harris – Team Lotus	5th	4th	
7/7/1963	FJ Race Part 1	Charade	12	Lotus 27	Ron Harris – Team Lotus	4th	2nd	
7/7/1963	FJ Race Part 2	Charade	12	Lotus 27	Ron Harris – Team Lotus	2nd	3rd	
7/7/1963	FJ Race Aggregate	Charade	29	Lotus 27	Ron Harris – Team Lotus		2nd	

Date	Race	Circuit	No	Car	Entered by	Qualified	Race Result	Notes
20/7/1963	FJ Race British GP Meeting	Silverstone	29	Lotus 27	Ron Harris – Team Lotus	6th	4th	
28/7/1963	FJ Race	Solitude	39	Lotus 27	Ron Harris – Team Lotus	2md	DNF	Retired after 3 laps with gearbox failure
24/8/1963	BARC FJ Championship	Goodwood	2	Lotus 27	Ron Harris – Team Lotus	5th	DNF	Retired after 17 laps with transmission failure
25/8/1963	GP de Zolder	Zolder	2	Lotus 27	Ron Harris – Team Lotus	4th	DNF	Retired after fly wheel failure
1/9/1963	Zandvoort Trophy	Zandvoort	4	Lotus 27	Ron Harris – Team Lotus	Unknown	DNF	Retired after a crash - multi car collision at start
8/9/1963	Italian Grand Prix	Monza	6	Lotus 25-Climax V8	Team Lotus	9th	13th	Classified but retired due to oil pressure on lap 73.
14/9/1963	Anglo-European Trophy Heat 1	Brands Hatch	3	Lotus 27	Ron Harris – Team Lotus	3rd	4th	
14/9/1963	Anglo-European Trophy Final	Brands Hatch	3	Lotus 27	Ron Harris – Team Lotus	4th	4th	
29/9/1963	Eifelpokal-Rennen	Nürburgring	3	Lotus 27	Ron Harris – Team Lotus	1st	2nd	Joint fastest lap
6/10/1963	Preis von Tirol	Innsbruck	3	Lotus 27	Ron Harris – Team Lotus	1st	2nd	10th L'Equipe rankings, 7th= Express & Star British Championship
21/3/1964	Sebring 12 Hours	Sebring	n/a	Ford Cortina Lotus	Team Lotus	n/a	DNA	
30/3/1964	News of the World International Sussex Trophy race	Goodwood	76	Lotus Elan	The Chequered Flag	Unknown	9th	
5/4/1964	GP de Pau Formula 2 race	Pau	4	Lotus 27	Ron Harris – Team Lotus	n/a	DNA	Car driven by Peter Arundell
5/4/1964	US Road Racing Club GT event	Pensacola, Florida	54	Ford Cortina Lotus	Alan Mann	Unknown	DNF	Retired due to oil leaking from the differential on lap 18
11/4/1964	National Open GT event	Oulton Park	89	Lotus Elan	The Chequered Flag	n/a	DNA	
12/4/1964	Syracuse Grand Prix	Syracuse	24	Lotus 25-Climax V8	Team Lotus	13th	DNF/3rd	Spence handed car over to Arundell, who finished 3rd. Spence retired Arundell's car with gearbox failure on lap 11
18/4/1964	Aintree 200 F2 Class	Aintree	25	Lotus 32	Ron Harris – Team Lotus	5th F2	1st F2	6th Overall, won class after 64 laps
18/4/1964	Aintree 200 F1 Non-Championship race	Aintree	25	Lotus 32-Cosworth S4	Ron Harris – Team Lotus	18th	6th	Won his class
26/4/1964	Eifelrennen Formula 2 race	Nürburgring	2	Lotus 32	Ron Harris – Team Lotus	4th	3rd	
2/5/1964	Silverstone International GT sportscar race	Silverstone	14	Lotus Elan	The Chequered Flag	n/a	DNA	Raced at Laguna Seca instead
3/5/1964	US Road Racing Club GT event	Laguna Seca	2	Ford Cortina Lotus	Alan Mann	11th	16th	7th in class
17/5/1964	Mallory Park GT race	Mallory Park	64	Lotus Elan	The Chequered Flag	Unknown	4th	
18/5/1964	London Trophy Heat 1 F2 race	Crystal Palace	3	Lotus 32	Ron Harris - Team Lotus	5th	DNF	Retired after engine failure 1st lap of 20
24/5/1964	GP von Berlin Part 1 F2 race	AVUS	9	Lotus 32	Ron Harris – Team Lotus	7th	DNF	Retired after 4 laps with mechanical failure
24/5/1964	GP von Berlin Part 2 F2 race	AVUS	9	Lotus 32	Ron Harris – Team Lotus		DNS	
24/5/1964	GP von Berlin Aggregate	AVUS	9	Lotus 32	Ron Harris – Team Lotus		DNF	
31/5/1964	1000km Nürburgring	Nürburgring	128	Lotus Elan	Ian Walker Racing	Unknown	DNS	
14/6/1964	Roskilde Ring Touring Car Event Heat 1	Roskilde		Ford Cortina Lotus	Team Lotus		2nd	
14/6/1964	Roskilde Ring Touring Car Event Heat 1	Roskilde		Ford Cortina Lotus	Team Lotus		1st	
28/6/1964	US Road Racing Championship Saloon car race	Watkins Glen		Ford Cortina Lotus	Team Lotus/English Fordline Operations	Unknown	7th	2nd in class
28/6/1964	US Road Racing Club GT event	Watkins Glen	12	Ford Cortina Lotus	Team Lotus	13th	7th	
5/7/1964	GP de Reims F2 race	Reims	6	Lotus 32	Ron Harris – Team Lotus	7th	3rd	
11/7/1964	British Grand Prix	Brands Hatch	2	Lotus 25-Climax V8	Team Lotus	13th	9th	
19/7/1964	Solitude F1 Grand Prix	Solitude	8	Lotus 25-Climax V8	Team Lotus	6th	DNF	Retired after 4 laps with steering failure which led to accident
2/8/1964	German Grand Prix	Nürburgring	2	Lotus 33-Climax V8	Team Lotus	17th	8th	
3/8/1964	The Slip Molyslip Trophy for saloon cars	Brands Hatch	147	Ford Cortina Lotus	Team Lotus	30th	DNF	Broken wheel on lap 30
3/8/1964	British Eagle Trophy F2 race	Brands Hatch	49	Lotus 32	Ron Harris – Team Lotus	12th	11th	
3/8/1964	International Guards Trophy meeting - GT2.5 class	Brands Hatch	110	Lotus Elan	The Chequered Flag	Unknown	2nd	
9/8/1964	GP di Pergusa Heat 2 F2 race	Pergusa	20	Lotus 32	Ron Harris – Team Lotus	1st	1st	Won after 20 laps, 96.14km. Also took joint fastest lap
9/8/1964	GP di Pergusa Final F2 race	Pergusa	20	Lotus 32	Ron Harris – Team Lotus	5th	6th	
16/8/1964	Mediterranean Grand Prix	Pergusa	6	Lotus 25-Climax V8	Team Lotus	5th	5th	Fastest lap of race and 1964.
23/8/1964	Austrian Grand Prix	Zeltweg	2	Lotus 33-Climax V8	Team Lotus	8th	DNF	Retired after 41 due to halfshaft failure
29/8/1964	29th International Tourist Trophy race - Grand Touring 2000 cc class	Goodwood	56	Lotus Elan	The Chequered Flag	Unknown	1st	Won after 21 laps, 92.946km at an average of 159.280kph
6/9/1964	Italian Grand Prix	Monza	10	Lotus 33-Climax V8	Team Lotus	8th	6th	
13/9/1964	GP d'Albi F2 race	Albi	3	Lotus 32	Ron Harris – Team Lotus	7th	DNF	Retired after engine failure lap 36 of 85
19/9/1964	International Gold Cup F2 race	Oulton Park	3	Lotus 32	Ron Harris – Team Lotus	12th	4th	
19/9/1964	Oulton Park Gold Cup Saloon car race	Oulton Park	81	Ford Cortina Lotus	Team Lotus	Unknown	DNF	Tyre burst on lap 13
26/9/1964	Vanwall Trophy F2	Snetterton	53	Lotus 32	Ron Harris – Team Lotus	1st	5th	Classified, but suffered misfiling engine

The Chaparral 2F at the 1967 BOAC 500, Brands Hatch. *John Spence*

Date	Race	Circuit	No	Car	Entered by	Qualified	Race Result	Notes
27/9/1964	GP de l'Ile de France F2 race	Montlhéry	10	Lotus 32	Ron Harris – Team Lotus	n/a	DNA	Car driven by Brian Hart
4/8/1964	United States Grand Prix	Watkins Glen	2	Lotus 33-Climax V8	Team Lotus	6th	7th/DNF	This was the last ever Formula One race in which drivers shared the same car. Car shared by Jim Clark. Clark entered the pits on lap 50, swapped cars and finished in 7th when he ran out of fuel. Spence carried on in Clark's faulty car until lap 54 until he retired due to fuel injection failure
4/10/1964	Coupe de Salon saloon car race	Montlhéry		Ford Cortina Lotus	Team Lotus		2nd	
11/10/1964	Riverside 200 miles	Riverside	n/a	Lotus 30	Team Lotus	n/a	DNA	
25/10/1964	Mexican Grand Prix	Mexico City	2	Lotus 25-Climax V8	Team Lotus	5th	4th	
12/12/1964	Rand Grand Prix Heat 2	Kyalami	2	Lotus 33-Climax V8	Team Lotus	2nd	DNF	Retired after 26 laps due to broken rose joint
12/12/1964	Rand Grand Prix Heat 1	Kyalami	2	Lotus 33-Climax V8	Team Lotus	2nd	2nd	
1/1/1965	South African Grand Prix	East London	6	Lotus 33-Climax V8	Team Lotus	4th	4th	
13/3/1965	Race of Champions Heat 2	Brands Hatch	6	Lotus 33-Climax V8	Team Lotus	3rd	1st	Won after 80 laps, 341.181km at average speed of 155.44kph
13/3/1965	Race of Champions Heat 1	Brands Hatch	6	Lotus 33-Climax V8	Team Lotus	3rd	3rd	
20/3/1965	BARC 200 F2 race	Silverstone	20	Lotus 32	Ron Harris – Team Lotus	10th	N/A	Race cancelled – flooded track
3/4/1965	Spring Trophy F2 race	Oulton Park	6	Lotus 32	Ron Harris – Team Lotus	n/a	DNA	Car driven by Brian Hart
4/4/1965	Syracuse Grand Prix	Syracuse	24	Lotus 33-Climax V8	Team Lotus	6th	DNF	Retired after 44 laps after an accident
10/4/1965	Autocar Trophy Part 1 F2 race	Snetterton	14	Lotus 32	Ron Harris – Team Lotus	11h	DNF	Retired after a crash on lap 1
10/4/1965	Autocar Trophy Part 2 F2 race	Snetterton	14	Lotus 32	Ron Harris – Team Lotus		DNS	
19/4/1965	Glover Trophy	Goodwood	6	Lotus 33-Climax V8	Team Lotus	4th	DNS	Fuel injection failure on the grid, did not start the race
25/4/1965	Eifelrennen Formula 2 race	Nürburgring	1	Lotus 35	Ron Harris – Team Lotus	1st	3rd	
15/5/1965	BRDC International Trophy	Silverstone	5	Lotus 33-Climax V8	Team Lotus	5th	3rd	
15/5/1965	BRDC International Trophy saloon car race	Silverstone	31	Ford Cortina Lotus	Team Lotus	4th	3rd	
7/6/1965	London Trophy Part 1 F2 race	Crystal Palace	16	Lotus 35	Ron Harris – Team Lotus	6th	8th	
7/6/1965	London Trophy Part 2 F2 race	Crystal Palace	16	Lotus 35	Ron Harris – Team Lotus	8th	7th	
7/6/1965	London Trophy Aggregate	Crystal Palace	16	Lotus 35	Ron Harris – Team Lotus		7th	
13/6/1965	Belgian Grand Prix	Spa	18	Lotus 33-Climax V8	Team Lotus	12th	7th	
27/6/1965	French Grand Prix	Charade	8	Lotus 33-Climax V8	Team Lotus	10th	7th	

Appendix: Race Results

Date	Race	Circuit	No	Car	Entered by	Qualified	Race Result	Notes
4/7/1965	GP de Reims F2 race	Reims	8	Lotus 35	Ron Harris - Team Lotus	16th	10th	
10/7/1965	British Grand Prix	Silverstone	6	Lotus 33-Climax V8	Team Lotus	6th	4th	
11/7/1965	GP de Rouen F2 race	Rouen	8	Lotus 35	Ron Harris - Team Lotus	11th	Classified 12th	Retired after a crash on lap 29 of 46
18/7/1965	Dutch Grand Prix	Zandvoort	8	Lotus 25-Climax V8	Team Lotus	8th	8th	
1/8/1965	German Grand Prix	Nürburgring	2	Lotus 33-Climax V8	Team Lotus	6th	DNF	Retired after 8 laps with transmission failure
8/8/1965	Kanonloppet F2 race	Karlskoga	4	Lotus 35	Ron Harris - Team Lotus	8th	4th	
10/8/1965	Guards Trophy	Brands Hatch		Ford Cortina Lotus	Team Lotus	n/a	DNS	Only took part in practice
15/8/1965	Mediterranean Grand Prix	Pergusa	8	Lotus 33-Climax V8	Team Lotus	2nd	DNF	Retired after 26 laps after an accident
22/8/1965	200 miles of Zeltweg	Zeltweg	2	Lotus 40	Team Lotus	1st	DNF	Retired due to overheating engine
30/8/1965	International Guards Trophy meeting	Brands Hatch	9	Lotus 40	Team Lotus	n/a	DNA	Raced in F2 race instead
30/8/1965	British Eagle Trophy F2 race	Brands Hatch	61	Lotus 35	Ron Harris - Team Lotus	6th	7th	
12/9/1965	Italian Grand Prix	Monza	26	Lotus 33-Climax V8	Team Lotus	8th	11th/DNF	Classified but retired due to an alternator problem on lap 62
18/9/1965	International Gold Cup F2 race	Oulton Park	5	Lotus 35	Ron Harris - Team Lotus	6th	DNF	Retired after a crash lap 23 of 40
26/9/1965	GP d'Albi F2 race	Albi	2	Lotus 35	Ron Harris - Team Lotus	8th	6th	
3/10/1965	United States Grand Prix	Watkins Glen	6	Lotus 33-Climax V8	Team Lotus	4th	DNF	Retired after 9 laps with engine failure
24/10/1965	Mexican Grand Prix	Mexico City	6	Lotus 33-Climax V8	Team Lotus	6th	3rd	
6/11/1965	9 Hours of Kyalami	Kyalami	7	Ferrari 250 LM	David Piper Auto Racing	7th*	7th	Co-drove with John Love. Cars started as a 'Le Mans start' in order of entry list number
4/12/1965	Rand Grand Prix	Kyalami	2	Lotus 33-Climax V8	Scuderia Scribante	n/a	DNS	Withdrawn before practice
1/1/1966	South African Grand Prix	East London	1	Lotus 33-Climax V8	Team Lotus	2nd	1st	Won after 60 laps, 234.592km at average speed of 157.32kph
11/4/1966	BARC Goodwood International Lavant Cup	Goodwood	143	Parnell-BRM	Reg Parnell (Racing)	Unknown	1st	Won after 21 laps, 80.467km at average speed of 157.362kph
24/4/1966	GP de Barcelona F2 race	Montjuic	7	Matra MS5	Tyrrell Racing Organisation	10th	DNF	Retired after a crash lap 31 of 60 avoiding a spectator
14/5/1966	BRDC International Trophy	Silverstone	12	Lotus 33-BRM V8	Reg Parnell (Racing)	4th	DNF	Retired after 5 Laps with engine failure
22/5/1966	Monaco Grand Prix	Monte Carlo	6	Lotus 33-BRM V8	Reg Parnell (Racing)	12th	DNF	Retired after 34 laps with suspension failure
30/5/1966	Anerley Trophy	Crystal Palace	80	Parnell-BRM	Reg Parnell (Racing)	1st	1st	Won after 20 laps, 45.062km
5/5/1966	1000km Nürburgring	Nürburgring	49	Ford GT40	Vixen Investments Ltd	17th	12th	Co-drove with Richard Bond
12/6/1966	Belgian Grand Prix	Spa	16	Lotus 33-BRM V8	Reg Parnell (Racing)	7th	DNF	Retired on the 1st lap after an accident
19/6/1966	Le Mans 24 Hours	Le Mans	11	Ford MKII	Holman & Moody	n/a	DNA	
2/7/1966	GP de Reims F2 race	Reims	6	Lotus 44	Ron Harris - Team Lotus	13th	4th	
3/7/1966	French Grand Prix	Reims	32	Lotus 33-BRM V8	Reg Parnell (Racing)	10th	DNF	Retired after 8 laps with a broken clutch
9/7/1966	Martini Trophy	Silverstone	1	Parnell-BRM	Reg Parnell (Racing)	Unknown	2nd	
16/7/1966	British Grand Prix	Silverstone	17	Lotus 33-BRM V8	Reg Parnell (Racing)	9th	DNF	Retired after 15 laps with an oil leak
24/7/1966	Dutch Grand Prix	Zandvoort	32	Lotus 33-BRM V8	Reg Parnell (Racing)	12th	5th	
7/8/1966	German Grand Prix	Nürburgring	15	Lotus 33-BRM V8	Reg Parnell (Racing)	13th	DNF	Retired after 12 laps with alternator failure
29/8/1966	International Guards Trophy meeting	Brands Hatch	38	Parnell-BRM	Reg Parnell (Racing)	n/a	DNA	
4/9/1966	Italian Grand Prix	Monza	42	Lotus 33-BRM V8	Reg Parnell (Racing)	14th	5th	
11/9/1966	500km Zeltweg	Zeltweg	3	Ford GT40	Nick Cussons	6th	DNF	Co-drove with Nick Cussons. Retired after engine overheated and caught fire
17/9/1966	Oulton Park Gold Cup	Oulton Park	11	Lotus 33-BRM V8	Reg Parnell (Racing)	7th	DNF	Retired after 25 laps with a broken clutch
2/10/1966	United States Grand Prix	Watkins Glen	18	Lotus 33-BRM V8	Reg Parnell (Racing)	12th	DNF	Retired after 74 laps with ignition failure
23/10/1966	Mexican Grand Prix	Mexico City	18	Lotus 33-BRM V8	Reg Parnell (Racing)	11th	DNS	Car damaged in practice, unable to repair car
5/11/1966	9 Hours of Kyalami	Kyalami	8	Ford GT40	Bernard White	Unknown	DNF	Co-drove with David Hobbs. Retired after 174 laps with crownwheel and pinion failure
2/1/1967	South African Grand Prix	Kyalami	6	BRM P83 H16	Owen Racing Organisation	13th	DNF	Retired after 31 laps with an oil leak
5/2/1967	24 Hours of Daytona	Daytona	15	Chaparral 2F	Chaparral Cars	2nd	DNF	Co-drove with Phil Hill. Retired after 93 laps from suspension damage sustained in an accident
12/3/1967	Race of Champions Heat 1	Brands Hatch	15	BRM P83 H16	Reg Parnell (Racing)	8th	5th	
12/3/1967	Race of Champions Heat 2	Brands Hatch	15	BRM P83 H16	Reg Parnell (Racing)	5th	7th	
27/3/1967	BARC 200 F2 race (Wills Trophy)	Silverstone	38	Lotus 33	Reg Parnell (Racing)	13th	9th	
1/4/1967	12 Hours of Sebring	Sebring	6	Chaparral 2F	Chaparral Cars	2nd	DNF	Co-drove with Jim Hall. Retired after 145 laps with differential problems
9/4/1967	GP de Barcelona F2 race	Montjuic	10	Lotus 25/33	Reg Parnell (Racing)	n/a	DNA	
15/4/1967	Daily Express Spring Cup Heat 1	Oulton Park	4	BRM P83 H16	Reg Parnell (Racing)	5th	3rd	
15/4/1967	Daily Express Spring Cup Heat 2	Oulton Park	4	BRM P83 H16	Reg Parnell (Racing)	3rd	6th	
15/4/1967	Daily Express Spring Cup Final	Oulton Park	4	BRM P83 H16	Reg Parnell (Racing)	6th	6th	
25/4/1967	1000km Monza	Monza	1	Chaparral 2F	Chaparral Cars	1st	DNF	Co-drove with Phil Hill. Retired due to driveshaft failure
29/4/1967	BRDC International Trophy	Silverstone	11	BRM P261 V8	Reg Parnell (Racing)	3rd	6th	
1/5/1967	1000km Spa	Spa	1	Chaparral 2F	Chaparral Cars	1st	DNF	Co-drove with Phil Hill. Retired after gearbox failure
7/5/1967	Monaco Grand Prix	Monte Carlo	5	BRM P83 H16	Owen Racing Organisation	12th	6th	
14/5/1967	Guards International Trophy Final F2 race	Mallory Park	12	Lotus 33	Reg Parnell (Racing)	5th	DNF	Retired after 22 laps with fuel injection failure
14/5/1967	Guards International Trophy Heat 1 F2 race	Mallory Park	12	Lotus 33	Reg Parnell (Racing)	7th	5th	
21/5/1967	Syracuse Grand Prix	Syracuse	22	BRM P261 V8	Reg Parnell (Racing)	4th	DNF	Retired after 23 laps with oil pressure
28/5/1967	1000km Nürburgring	Nürburgring	4	Chaparral 2F	Chaparral Cars	1st	DNF	Co-drove with Phil Hill. Retired after 10 laps due to gearbox failure
29/5/1967	London Trophy F2 race	Brands Hatch	6	Lotus 33	Reg Parnell (Racing)	9th	9th	
4/6/1967	Dutch Grand Prix	Zandvoort	10	BRM P83 H16	Owen Racing Organisation	12th	8th	

Mike in the BRM at the 1967 German Grand Prix. *Press Photos Ltd/John Spence*

Date	Race	Circuit	No	Car	Entered by	Qualified	Race Result	Notes
11/6/1967	Le Mans 24 Hours	Le Mans	7	Chaparral 2F	Chaparral Cars	2nd	DNF	Co drove with Phil Hill. Retired after 225 laps with a broken transmission oil seal
18/6/1967	Belgian Grand Prix	Spa	12	BRM P83 H16	Owen Racing Organisation	11th	5th	
2/7/1967	French Grand Prix	Bugatti Circuit, Le Mans	11	BRM P83 H16	Owen Racing Organisation	12th	DNF	Retired after 9 laps with halfshaft failure
15/7/1967	British Grand Prix	Silverstone	4	BRM P83 H16	Owen Racing Organisation	11th	DNF	Retired after 44 laps with failed ignition
30/7/1967	BOAC 500 6 Hours of Brands Hatch	Brands Hatch	1	Chaparral 2F	Chaparral Cars	3rd	1st	Co drove with Phil Hill. Won after 211 laps, 899.863km at an average speed of 149.797kph
6/8/1967	German Grand Prix	Nürburgring	12	BRM P83 H16	Owen Racing Organisation	11th	DNF	Retired after 3 laps with differential failure
27/8/1967	Canadian Grand Prix	Mosport	16	BRM P83 H16	Owen Racing Organisation	10th	5th	
3/9/1967	6 Hours of Brno Race Meeting	Brno	n/a	BRM P83 H16	Owen Racing Organisation	n/a	n/a	Reliability run in between two Formula Three races. Broke lap record with 4min 44.8sec which was average of 176kmh. Lap record stood for five years
10/9/1967	Italian Grand Prix	Monza	36	BRM P83 H16	Owen Racing Organisation	12th	5th	
17/9/1967	Can-Am Challenge Cup	Bridgehampton	22	McLaren Elva M1B	Ecurie Soucy Racing Team	14th	DNF	Retired after 47 laps with a broken gearbox
23/9/1967	Can-Am Challenge Cup (Player's 200)	Mosport	22	McLaren Elva M1B	Ecurie Soucy Racing Team	4th	3rd	
1/10/1967	United States Grand Prix	Watkins Glen	8	BRM P83 H16	Owen Racing Organisation	13th	DNF	Retired after 35 laps with engine failure
15/10/1967	Can-Am Challenge Cup	Laguna Seca	22	McLaren Elva M1B	Ecurie Soucy Racing Team	6th	DNF	Retired after 26 laps due to brake failure
22/10/1967	Mexican Grand Prix	Mexico City	8	BRM P83 H16	Owen Racing Organisation	11th	5th	
29/10/1967	Can-Am Challenge Cup	Riverside	22	McLaren Elva M1B	Ecurie Soucy Racing Team	11th	5th	
4/11/1967	9 Hours of Kyalami	Kyalami	5	Lola T70	Sid Taylor	Unknown	DNF	Co-drove with Frank Gardner. Retired after split fuel tank after collision
12/11/1967	Can-Am Challenge Cup	Las Vegas	22	McLaren Elva M1B	Ecurie Soucy Racing Team	8th	3rd	
1/1/1968	South African Grand Prix	Kyalami	12	BRM P115 H16	Owen Racing Organisation	13th	DNF	Retired after 7 laps with fuel system failure
17/3/1968	Race of Champions	Brands Hatch	12	BRM P126 V12	Owen Racing Organisation	2nd	DNF	Retired after 18 laps with oil line failure
7/4/1968	BOAC 500 6 Hours of Brands Hatch	Brands Hatch	34	Ford F3L	Alan Mann	2nd	DNF	Co-drove with Bruce McLaren. Retired after 66 laps with driveshaft failure
25/4/1968	BRDC International Trophy	Silverstone	7	BRM P126 V12	Owen Racing Organisation	2nd	DNF	Retired after 40 laps with timing gear failure
7/5/1968	Indianapolis 500	Indianapolis	30	Lotus 56 Gas Turbine	STP Oil Treatment/ Team Lotus	n/a	DNS	Killed in practice
7/5/1968	Indianapolis 500	Indianapolis	60	Lotus 56 Gas Turbine	STP Oil Treatment/ Team Lotus	n/a	DNS	Killed in practice
19/5/1968	1000km of Nürburgring	Nürburgring	8	Ford F3L	Alan Mann	n/a	DNS	Killed 12 days previously

Bibliography

BOOKS

50 Years of British Grand Prix Drivers by Peter Scherer. Published in 1999 by TFM Publishing.

All Set From a CERT by Jim Meikle. Published in 1962 by Fraser Meikle.

As it Happened – Reflections on my Life by John Spence. Published in 2019 by John Spence.

BRM Volume 3 – The Saga of British Racing Motors – Monocoque V8 Cars 1963-1969 by Doug Nye with Tony Rudd. Published in 2008 by Motor Racing Publications.

Cars in Profile – No. 4 – The Chaparral 2, 2D and 2F by Pete Lyons. Published in 1972 by Profile Publications.

Chaparral by Richard Falconer with Doug Nye. Published in 1992 by Motorbooks International.

A Chequered Life: Graham Warner and the Chequered Flag by Richard Heseltine. Published in 2013 by Veloce Publishing.

Colin Chapman: Inside the Innovator by Karl Ludvigsen. Published in 2010 by Haynes Publishing.

Elva – The Cars, The People, The History by Janos Wimpffen. Published in 2011 by David Bull Publishing.

Ford GT – Then and Now by Adrian Streather. Published in 2006 by Veloce Publishing.

Ian Walker – The Man and His Cars by Julian Balme. Published in 2012 by Coterie Press.

It was Fun! by Tony Rudd. Published in 1993 by Patrick Stephens.

Men at the Wheel by Peter Miller. Published in 1963 by BT Batsford.

Piers Courage: Last of the Gentlemen Racers by Adam Cooper. Published in 2003 by Haynes Publishing.

Tales from the Toolbox by Michael Oliver. Published in 2009 by Veloce Publishing.

Team Lotus – The Indianapolis Years by Andrew Ferguson. Published in 1996 by Patrick Stephens.

The British at Indianapolis by Ian Wagstaff. Published in 2010 by Veloce Publishing.

Theme Lotus by Doug Nye. Published in 1978 by Motor Racing Publications.

The Story of Lotus 1961-1971 – Growth of a Legend by Doug Nye. Published in 1972 by Motor Racing Publications.

Williams: The legendary story of Frank Williams and his F1 team in their own words by Maurice Hamilton. Published in 2009 by Ebury Press.

NEWSPAPERS

Burlington (North Carolina) Daily Times News, 18 February 1965.

The Chicago Tribune, 2 September 1968.

Coventry Evening Telegraph, 5 April 1968.

The Indianapolis Star, 7 May 1968.

Maidenhead Advertiser, 14 January 1966, 11 March 1966, 13 May 1966, 27 May 1966, 4 August 1967, 10 May 1968.

The Miami Herald, 27 May 1965.

Montreal Gazette, 10 November 1967.

The Observer Newspaper, 23 May 1965 (by Alan Brinton).

The Pensacola News Journal, 3 April 1964 (Al Padgett column).

Reading Evening Post, 29 October 1965, 2h February 1966 (by Michael Nicks), 21 April 1966 (Nicks), 9 May 1966 (Nicks), 8 May 1968 (by Clive Pulman), 9 May 1968, 14 May 1968, 6 August 1968.

Sutton and Croydon Guardian, 16 December 2012.

Winnipeg Free Press, 19 August 1967.

Mike in the paddock before the start of a Formula 2 race. *Peter Darley*

Mike Spence and Phil Hill wave to the crowd at the BOAC 500, 1967.

Peter Darley

Mike at the Belgian Grand Prix, 1965. *Etienne Bourguignon*

MAGAZINES

Autosport Magazine – 4 August 1961 (Commander Yorke Trophy race report), Mike Spence – A profile by Bill Gavin, March 26 1965, Obituary – 17 May 1968, Funeral Report – 24 May 1968.

Car Magazine – British Grand Prix preview edition, July 1965.

Classic Cars Magazine – interview with Bob Sparshott by Ivan Ostroff, 1 March 2020.

Formula Junior Historic Racing Association magazine – Paul Emery and the Emeryson Formula Juniors – Graham Rabagliati, 2020.

Grand Prix Plus – Look Back: Mike Spence by David Tremayne, Issue 18 , March 24 2008.

Motor Racing magazine – Twenty Questions, December 1967.

Motoring News – race report of International Trophy, 2 May 1968.

Motor Sport magazine – The BOAC 500 by Denis Jenkinson, September 1967; The Cars of Paul Emery by Mike Lawrence, March 1985; Formula Junior – 25 years on by Mike Lawrence, January 1985; From the Archives with Doug Nye, July 2013; Italian Grand Prix 1963 report by Denis Jenkinson, November 1963, Looking back at Mike Spence by Alan Henry, August 1986; Looking back at Peter Arundell by Mike Lawrence, July 1984; Looking back at Tim Parnell, by Alan Henry, January 1985; Lunch with Hugh Dibley by Colin Goodwin, January 2018; Lunch with The Team Lotus mechanics by Simon Taylor, August 2015, Mike Spence: An Unrewarded Talent by David Tremayne, July 1997; Mike Spence: The Cruel Fate of 1968 by Paul Fearnley, 10th May 2018; Phil Hill and the Chaparral 2F by Gordon Kirby, 24th January 2011; The Quiet Man by Paul Fearnley, June 2005.

Shell Motorsport Profiles – Number Six: Mike Spence. Published by Shell International Petroleum Company, 1967.

Small Car Magazine – The Hustlers: Mike Spence by Max Le Grand, September 1964.

Speedworld International – International Trophy race report by Gregor Grant, 4 May 1968; Mike Spence Obituary by Gregor Grant, 11 May 1968.

WEBSITES

www.oldracingcars.com

www.open-wheels.com – Faces of the 500 by Tanner Watkins, 3 November 2017

www.sports cartv.net

www.tentenths.com

www.the-fastlane.co.uk/formula2/index.html

www.touringcarracing.net

Index